Surviving Hollywood North

Crew Confessions from an Insider

by
Ellie Presner

July 11/18, Montreal
To cousin Allan, thanks so
much for making me your guest
at your show! Please accept
this little token of my appreciation!
♡♡♡
Ellie

ISBN: 978-0-9695957-3-1
Surviving Hollywood North:
Crew Confessions from an Insider

Cover design by Select-O-Grafix, LLC

Published by Jerell Publishing
crossedeyesanddottedtees.wordpress.com

For film lovers everywhere

Table of Contents

FOREWORD

I became a script coordinator in the '90s on films and TV series by accident. Darn good thing I was a quick learner, as I soon discovered that film productions consist of a zillion moving parts, with hordes of incredibly talented people all focused on one task: making something amazing out of words on paper: a *script*. It's magic. I loved it! Well, *most* of it.

Read on and rejoice, or weep, as required.

DISCLAIMER

All the events in this account really happened as I experienced them. Several names have been changed to protect the innocent or guilty, as the case may be.

I apologize for any inadvertent errors or omissions.

PROLOGUE

On a warm spring afternoon in May 1996, the phone rang. Well okay, it rang a lot of times in May 1996, but this was different.

It was a call from a production coordinator I'd worked with previously, Jacqueline Marleau – yet another fabulously bilingual film-crew member, so prevalent in our multicultural city, Montreal, Quebec.

Her timing is excellent, I thought! Here I am, right between two seasons of *Space Cases,* and she's no doubt calling about a feature for me. It'll fit in perfectly!

After our warm greetings, she says, "So Ellie, maybe you heard, there's this show called *Hysteria* I'm working on."

I tell her that's great, her timing is excellent.

"Well actually, I'm not really calling for you to work on *Hysteria.* Someone's already doing the script revisions."

"Oh," I say, deflated, yet curious. "So…?"

"What I'm really calling about is this. We have an actor on the show – do you know of Patrick McGoohan?"

Is the pope Catholic, I think to myself. But I don't say it, because Jacqueline, like most French-speaking Quebecois, is probably Catholic, and I don't want to offend her. It's also quite possible that she herself had not heard of Patrick McGoohan, since the French and English cultures were often quite separate. (The noted Canadian author, Hugh MacLennan, wrote a much-lauded book in 1945 – *Two Solitudes* – about how insulated the lives of French and English people in Quebec usually were from one another. In that light, perhaps she thought I had never heard of him either.)

In any case, my response to her question was: *"Of course!"* I was a little excited, what can I tell you. Everyone – well, every female of a certain age who had ever watched the 1960s cult TV hits, *Secret Agent* (aka *Danger Man*) or *The Prisoner* – had nursed a crush on him, he of the handsome face and a voice of such authority that it rang out with a clarion force that – oops, I'm getting carried away here.

Right, so now Jacqueline says, "Well Ellie, Mr. McGoohan asked me if I knew anyone who could help him out with his script. Would you be interested?"

"His script?" *His* script? I was all a-quiver with attention. If I'd been a cat, my ears would've been pricked forward, and my whiskers too. (Only later did I learn that the script he was writing was for a feature film, a sequel to his classic '60s show, *The Prisoner.*)

"Yes," she said. "He's writing his own script, and he says he needs someone to help him, to work with him, because he doesn't have a computer here." Oh.

"Listen, he's right here, he can explain it to you, so can you talk to him now?"

My knees turned to jelly. Was I dreaming?

"Hello, Ellie!!!" his voice boomed in my

ear. "How are you?" It was as familiar as yesterday. It was, unmistakably, the voice of Number Six, the *Prisoner* himself. Crisp, clipped, sublime diction. And loud. Right. In. My. Left. Ear.

My breathing quickened.

"H-hi, uh, Patrick?" Wait, I thought, was that presumptuous? She called him "Mr. McGoohan" before. What if he-

"Yes, well Ellie, Jacqueline here tells me that you're a *whiz* on the computer.

Is that right?" That emphasis on *whiz*. I could barely breathe now.

I was in a daze. All I remember from the rest of our short conversation was that I agreed to go to his hotel – the Ritz-Carlton – on Sunday morning at 10 a.m., and to bring my laptop. I didn't *have* a laptop. But I damn well knew I would *very* soon be renting one ("Never say *no*," aka "Always say *yes*").

I ended up renting one from a friend of my daughter's; it was called an "Outbound," and was a rare Macintosh clone. I remember its kangaroo logo, although it was not an Australian company. I tried it out, and it filled the bill. It even came with a case, woo-hoo! I was set to go.

For the next couple of days, I forced myself to calm down, realizing I'd be useless if I went there and met him while huddled up in a nervous ball of shivering slime. I reminded myself that I had a fair bit of experience under my belt now, on a variety of shows, with different software and people with all their quirks. Soon I was about to meet one of the quirkiest of them all.

****

I dress carefully, as if for a job interview. In a way, that's what it is, isn't it?

Except that he's already under the impression that I'm super-duper at script stuff, so hey, who am I to argue with him?

One last look in the mirror: I figure I look cool yet casual, able yet arty.

I practise breathing deeply, nice and easy, and decide to just try and treat him as, well, a colleague. We'd be in this together, wouldn't we? As equals.

Sunday, 9:55 a.m. The doorman ushers me through the gilded doors of Montreal's storied hotel jewel, the Ritz Carlton. Home of Elizabeth Taylor's first marriage ceremony with Richard Burton, 1964. And now: Ellie Presner and Patrick McGoohan's work on a *Prisoner* movie script, 1996!

I'm at the door to his suite. I knock, with as much confidence as I can muster.

The door opens…

PART ONE – FALLING
INTO THE BIZ

My first gig was a hand-me-up from my son.

During the 1990s, the "Hollywood North" moniker fit Montreal, no question. Well, to us Montrealers, that is. Vancouver and Toronto may have disagreed, sure, but we were very proud of the quantity and quality of our film and TV work – in both English and French, no less.

Our fair city hosted dozens of production companies. At any time, a slew of local and American movies and TV series kept our skilled crews busy. Top-notch talent plus our low, low, dollar: U.S. filmmakers simply couldn't lose by shooting here. (In 1995, every U.S. dollar could buy you $1.37 CAD.)

Whenever I tell someone I toiled in the "trenches" of the film biz, I mean that I worked in the production offices of more than sixty shows during the '90s as a script coordinator – on mini-series, theatrical feature films, TV series, and MOWs (movies of the week, aka "Disease of the Week" or made-for-TV movies). My complete filmography appears in the Appendix.

The first time

How did I get into this, anyway – a whole decade as a script coordinator – despite the fact that my training and prior career had focused on social work? How the heck did *that* happen? Well, you could say: by accident. It was the summer of 1991. I was at loose ends, having just finished a contract at a community centre. I was unsure what to do next, but thanks must go to my son, Jeremy, who soon had to start classes at Concordia University.

Through a friend of a friend, he'd been given a part-time summer job – for a flat fee – of typing a script and inserting changes scrawled on some of its pages. It was a big undertaking, as it was twice the ordinary script length – over 300 pages, in fact (one page equals approximately one minute of screen time). It was to be a two-part TV mini-series. In any case, Jeremy had been typing away on this monster script on our little Mac SE, but now he had to figure out how on earth he could finish the job, and go to classes and do his assignments all at the same time.

Ta-daa! Enter mama Ellie! *I'll* type the script, I said, grinning from ear to ear. (It brought to mind the line from Mighty Mouse – "*Here* I come to save the *daaay!*") So that was how my name eventually got into the film credits as script coordinator on *Vendetta II: The New Mafia.* But what I thought would be a simple typing job turned out to be a lot more than that.

Okay, so what does a script coordinator do, anyway?

As I learned on future shows, the script would normally come to me typed in an electronic version (and often a hard copy as well). But my first gig was a tad more complicated. It came to us *only* on paper. So, Jeremy, my techie son, had typed it into our computer, using an early version of Word, while setting up macros for each script element.

What are these elements, you may ask? And what about Jeremy's macros, for that matter?

A script consists of specific parts, such as scene headings, dialogue, action, and so on. These same elements are repeated all the way through. If you create macros for them, it saves having to adjust the tabs and spaces for each different element. Just press Command-3, for example, and the cursor automatically will take you to the spot for the Character Name you want to type. Command-2 would take you to dialogue, and so on (if these are the instructions you gave for your macros).

If you've never seen a film script, here's a tiny sample of how it's formatted with the different elements:

FADE IN:

INT. LIVING ROOM - DAY

HEDY (46) and her mother,
SONIA (80), chat while playing
Scrabble.

> HEDY
> Ma, suppose you could
> travel anywhere you
> wanted to, I mean if
> money were no object.
> Where would you want to
> go?

Sonia has a doubtful look.
Long pause.

> HEDY (cont'd)
> And, if you didn't have
> this foot problem, if
> you could walk okay.
> Isn't there some place
> you would like to visit?

> SONIA
> (after a moment)
> Well, I suppose Israel.

CUT TO:

In this little Oscar-winner wannabe excerpt, we have:

- FADE IN: and CUT TO: are called Transitions. At the very end of a script, it would usually say FADE OUT, or FADE TO BLACK.
- INT. LIVING ROOM – DAY is the Scene Heading. (In a production script, i.e. shooting script, it would have a number, but in earlier drafts such as this one, the headings have no numbers yet.) Underlining is optional.
- "HEDY (46) and her mother, SONIA (80), chat while playing scrabble." – this is an Action element.
- HEDY and SONIA are the Character Names.
- The element "(after a moment)" is called, for obvious reasons, a Parenthetical.
- The "(cont'd)" after HEDY is *not* called a Parenthetical. It's referred to simply as a "Continued." A few years later it would automatically be inserted there by various amazing software programs that were developed, such as Final Draft or Screenwriter.
- The last element in this little script sample is the set of lines that the

characters are speaking, called, yes, Dialogue.

****

Just as these formatting elements are script "conventions," the typeface used is always the same: The monospaced Courier (or Courier New), 12 pt. regular. It resembles typewriter printing. If you ever see a script typed in any other font, or in italics, or bold, or coloured, or with butterflies and hearts and flowers on the page, you can bet it was not done by a professional.

Now comes the *really* tricky part.

Rainbow revisions

A script usually goes through a gazillion revisions. After the writer is satisfied with his/her draft, everyone on the production and their uncle/aunt, not to mention nephew/niece, feels they have a right to put in their two cents and suggest, no, *demand* changes. All agreed-upon changes have to be incorporated into the script in a new version. Each set of revisions – for there are many! – must be kept separate and made instantly recognizable by differently coloured pages. Guess whose job that is. Right!

I soon learned that after the first draft comes:

Revised (white)
Second Revised (white)
Third Revised (if necessary) (white)
Production Draft (sometimes called
Table Draft or Shooting Script) – pages
locked; scene numbers added. (white)
Pink
Blue
Yellow
Green
Goldenrod
Lilac
Salmon
Tan
Etc., until you run out of colours, at
which point you start all over again with
white, so you then have:
Double White
Double Pink
Etc., ad infinitum!

Different production houses may use
different colours, depending on what paper
was available or on sale the day the
production coordinator put in her order...
although the first few colours are almost always
universal.

The important point is that all these revised
versions must be kept in the computer as
separate files. Tech-savvy people will
understand me when I say that the "Save As"
command becomes your best friend. Thus, you

would end up with many files with names like BIRDPINK, BIRDBLUE, and BIRDYELL – back when I started, when computer file names could only be eight characters long, or BIRDING.doublepink when you could have longer names.

The reason you keep the older files is that film bigwigs have the infuriating habit of saying, days or weeks down the line, "You know… I think I liked that scene opening better in the Second Revised. Can you put it back?" This, after you're now on yellow pages! But luckily you saved it!

By the way, the answer to that question, "Can you put it back?" is always *yes*. In fact, your answer to anything in the film biz should always be a resounding *yes*. Unpleasantness can ensue from a *no*.

So, as I said, the script coordinator has to type into the script the new bits and pieces that all the aunts, uncles, nieces, nephews, various producers, directors, writers, studio execs, directors' girlfriends, nannies, etc., have passed along to you. These changes may be fed to you in a variety of ways:

- Fax (where the handwritten comments may be very faint and thus unreadable, or cut off, necessitating phone calls seeking clarification – good luck with that).
- Email – interestingly, not a big favourite yet in the 90s.

- Scribbled on napkins in a restaurant, entailing the necessity of differentiating the letter "o" from a coffee drop.
- Verbal instruction in person while peering over your shoulder as you're typing, making you nervous, so you make mistakes galore.
- Verbally on phone. (See next paragraph re accents!)
- Scrawled on the script itself.

It's up to you to decipher said scribbles and chicken scratches… and understand southern accents or Irish brogues over a crackly long-distance phone line. It's important that you get it right, too, or the hell to pay will come down on your head.

Along the revision route, you'll become best buddies with your liaison, who is the main person feeding you script changes. This person might be different from show to show or even within one show. It might be the director, an assistant director (AD), the production coordinator, the writer him- or herself, or a producer (or several *different* producers – who may contradict each other – which always adds to the fun)!

It should be emphasized here that if you don't like *change,* you sure won't make it in the film biz!

Meeting the director

As time went on, I was asked to continue my labours on the *Vendetta II* script – which I'd been working on at home – on site. The production office of the company, Filmline International, was located in Old Montreal – a popular film location, as a stand-in for European cities like London, Paris or Berlin.

The production manager, a friendly woman by the name of Nicole Hilaréguy, had sent a driver to pick me up and bring me there for the first time. A nice touch. She welcomed me and showed me to a small office set up with a desk and computer which would be my workstation.

I was just finishing getting settled and uploading the script file from my floppy disk onto the computer, when Nicole walked in with Ralph, the director. She introduced us and then left.

Now, I tend to be a neurotic worrier, but a funny thing happens whenever I encounter someone even more nervous than I am. I strangely become calmer, and inevitably end up soothing *them*. And that's exactly what happened with Ralph. An experienced director, writer and producer, the poor fellow was nevertheless very fretful about the script. The damn thing was now 343 pages long, which is impossible for a normal script, but as this was for a mini-series it was actually just about right. It was to be shot as two episodes.

The thing Ralph seemed most concerned about was whether or not I'd be able to generate A & B[1] pages correctly. "It's gonna be a dog's breakfast," he said, woefully. But I understood how to do them; I had seen a couple of other scripts by then. I tried to assuage his fears.

This gargantuan script generated a *lot* of A & B pages, but I was able to handle them. Ralph grew to trust me, and (some of) his worry lines faded.

And you get a script, and you get a script, and you...

It's a script coordinator's job to make sure that each new set of revisions is sent around to every person involved in the production.

Of course, we all realize that filmmaking is a collaborative effort. But it doesn't really sink in until you see the crew and cast lists, usually generated by the production coordinator. It's a heckuva lot of people. The bigger the production, the more people working on it, naturally. *Vendetta II* had a huge crew and castlist.

On some shows, it was my job to physically photocopy all the revised script pages and send them around to everybody. Sometimes the production secretary or office production assistant (PA) does it. It's an awful lot of

---

[1] For A & B pages, see Script Lore in the Appendix.

copying. Many trees have died in the service of the movie biz! Kudos to the industry for at least being early adopters of recycling.

Often, I would stuff the new pages in each crew member's "box" – usually a manila envelope tacked onto the wall with the person's name on it. There are usually a couple of rows of these near the entrance to the production office. Sometimes I would need to enlist the office driver or the services of a courier. However, it goes, everyone has to get the new pages.

First set visit

My *favourite* method of script distribution was personally delivering them, especially when it necessitated a trip to the location where they were filming.

This first show I worked on, *Vendetta II: The New Mafia,* involved shooting in a grassy suburb of Montreal on the spacious grounds of an elegant stone- walled museum/exhibit space, Stewart Hall. This was meant to be the estate or "compound" of the Mafia boss of the story.

On my way to find Marie, my liaison, who did continuity on the show, I passed by gleaming luxury cars in the long curving driveway, PAs dashing every which way, and a rather short middle-aged man who was talking to someone wearing a headset. The man looked familiar; it came to me eventually – it was Burt Young, who had played Rocky Balboa's slovenly brother-in-law in the Rocky series of movies. My first "brush with celebrity" ... well, not a "brush" really, more like a "sighting" from 30 feet away.

Clutching fat manila envelopes with the revised script pages I had prepared myself, I found Marie after asking a few crew members where she was. Since I had never met her, I didn't know what she looked like. My school French came in handy; most of the crew were bilingual francophones, including Marie herself.

We sat at a long table going over the changes. She asked me if I'd had lunch, and since I hadn't, she led me to the makeshift dining room. There were long tables and a ton of food set up buffet-style. I couldn't eat much, being rather nervous on my maiden trip to a set. But it was comforting to know that film companies made sure you never starved!

In fact, as I learned, they always *had* to feed you well, because most of the cast and crew worked very long hours. Provisions were also a-plenty at all the offices where I toiled over the years. There would always be a kitchen featuring lots of snacks, hot and cold drinks, fruit, protein bars, chocolate, you name it, all available for the noshing. Bagels were a big favourite here in Montreal, home of the best bagels in the world. (Okay, so I'm a teensy bit biased.)

Back at Stewart Hall, after the meeting and lunch with Marie, I found the PA who'd driven me out to the set, and he drove me back to the office. I felt like a real pro now. For me, at least, the rest of the show was a cinch.

PART TWO – ARE YOU AFRAID OF THE DARK?

Well, there was no goin' back to social work now! I was bitten by the intoxicating movie bug! The buzz of creativity along with the drama of deadlines made for a compelling mix. I loved the feeling of everyone pitching in to create one special thing, and to make it the best it can be. It's as though every crew member tossed a different delicious fruit into the bowl, and the end result was an amazing fruit salad!

A few months passed after *Vendetta*. I'd been doing some freelance editing work, when I got an auspicious phone call. After I said hello, a woman's voice intoned, ominously: "Are you afraid of the dark?"

Silence. I froze, perplexed. What was this, an obscene phone call, but from a woman? That's unusu–

"Hi Ellie," the voice chirped. "It's me, Nicole! Remember, from *Vendetta?*"

"Oh right!" I said, grinning, feeling a bit silly. She'd been the production manager on the show. Well, one of several PMs, actually. But I was still somewhat puzzled over her choice of conversation-starter.

"Are you afraid of the daaaaark?" She said it again, with an extra-eerie tone! Then she continued, "Ellie, are you available? I'd love it if you could come work on our show…"

"Uh, oh, um sure, I'd –"

"It's called *Are You Afraid of the Dark –*

it's a TV series. I'd like you to be the script coordinator."

WOW, I thought. I'd done just one show, and now a production manager thinks highly enough of me to want me again. I felt like Sally Field at the 1984 Oscars, after she won a Best Actress award for *Places in the Heart* and gushed, "You like me! Right now, you like me!" (She was often misquoted as, "You like me! You really like me!")

This was the moment I first realized that people working in the film business are like one big family. Just about everyone knows everyone, after working on many of the same shows time after time with a lot of the same crew. In that sense, the adage that "it's who you know" holds true. (Although, it does *not* apply if you do a sub-par job or are a difficult person with whom to work.)

In the same way, nepotism runs rampant in the industry. Even a casual look through the cast and crew credits after any movie or TV show will reveal some very familiar surnames. Chances are that, yes, that *is* so-and-so's son or daughter. There's no question that film doors open easily if you are a known quantity and do good work.

The challenge

I was brought aboard this wildly successful children's show – a co-production involving Cinar, Nickelodeon and YTV – mid-way through its second season, which consisted of 13 half-hour episodes. Up until now, the creator of the show (and frequent writer and director), D.J. MacHale, an easygoing, down-to-earth fellow, had apparently been taking care of all the script revisions himself. Finally, he decided to delegate this important task to – me! Well, via Nicole.

But I soon found out that there was, shall we say, a bit of a challenge: the script work was being done on an IBM PC, *not* a Mac, which I had at home and was used to – since 1988. I was terrified.

No problem, said Nicole to me on the phone. First of all, since I'd be working mostly at home on this one, she would have a PC brought over to my house. The "guys" would install it, no sweat! Nicole *never* saw a problem she couldn't fix, I was to learn. She had definitely learned the credo, *Always say yes!* It was no wonder her services were so much in demand, to this day, in fact. As I write this, I just saw her name in the credits as line producer on 2015's *Brooklyn,* starring Saoirse Ronan.

So, I learned a lot, in a very short amount of time. The scripts were in Word, which was essentially the same app on the PC as it was on the Mac. (There still wasn't any dedicated software for scripts that was widely available.) I did everything manually just as on *Vendetta* – respecting locked pages, generating A's and B's, all of it. Nicole had unwittingly done me a favour. She made me – let's see, not ambidextrous, not bilingual, no, more like bi-computeral. Maybe you can guess that I made up that word. You may borrow it.

Backstories and stories

After the behemoth script on *Vendetta II,* these little stories ran a way-more-manageable 30 pages on average, with names like *The Tale of the Super Specs, The Tale of Locker 22,* and *The Tale of the Midnight Ride.* The show had a really cute concept: every week a small group of the same kids would meet and sit around an evening campfire, and take turns telling scary ghost stories. They were fun to read on the page, and when I got to see a few episodes on tape, I was blown away by how well they were done, technically. Why, I was kind of scared myself!

The acting was excellent, too. It's well known in the Montreal acting community and beyond that this show launched many careers. Jay Baruchel, Elisha Cuthbert, Jacob Tierney, Emily Hampshire, Mia Kirshner and many other successful performers got their start on *Are You Afraid.*

Just as D.J. MacHale had a good eye for actors, he also had a good eye for stories. After I'd seen a number of his scripts, I thought it looked easy, so I tried my hand at writing one. Well, a treatment[2] for one... called *The Tale of the Antique Computer.* But it didn't pass muster

---

[2] A treatment is somewhere between an outline and a finished script, in both length and detail.

– it was too similar to something they'd already done (about a haunted typewriter; I hadn't seen it). Just for fun, I'm including it here. Knock yourself out!

THE TALE OF THE ANTIQUE COMPUTER

A treatment for a 30-minute teleplay

by

Ellie Presner

Aug. 14/93

Campfire setting: the story is introduced as an event that happened to a boy who tried to take a short cut to success.

Mark Tyler and his friend Kenny (both 12) walk to the tennis court, rackets in hand. Kenny asks Mark if he's done that history paper due in a few days. Kenny's already finished it, he's a real early bird. No, Mark admits he hasn't, and he's really worried: his typewriter's broken, his handwriting is terrible, what's he gonna *do*. He's doomed for sure. No, his dad can't afford a new typewriter, he can't afford *any*thing, now that he got laid off.

Mark's probably gonna flunk history, and dad will be so mad. What he *really* wishes he had is a computer, but... there's no way.

On the court, Mark and Kenny get down to playing tennis... sort of.

They're at a beginner's level, and that's being kind. One of Kenny's thwacked balls does a home run over the fence; it's Mark's turn to get it. Out of the court and around the side he goes, foraging in the bushes, in a crouch. It's hard to see the yellow ball among the yellow-green dense leaves, but finally he spots it – and – hey, what's this, lying next to it?

A wallet! A black leather wallet, just lying there, near the ball. Mark blinks, picks up the ball, then the wallet. He looks all around; he's hidden by shrubs... He opens the wallet and quickly rifles through it. To Kenny's impatient call of "what's taking so long!" he yells back – to buy time – that he's still looking for the ball, but thinks he sees it. The wallet holds – besides various credit and ID cards – two hundred dollars in bills. Wow! Used computer, anyone?! Mark unthinkingly shoves the entire wallet into his pocket; it's thin and light. As he emerges from the bushes and heads back to the court, he deliberately relaxes his demeanour. He's not going to tell Kenny about this. Kenny would never approve of what he plans to do...

When Mark arrives home, he goes straight to his room. He realizes now it was dumb to take the whole wallet when all he really needs is the money – which he just plans to, uh, *borrow*, really. He removes the bills and pockets them, then after looking around for a safe hiding place, shoves the wallet way in the back of a bottom drawer, behind some old model airplane kits.

He sits down with the yellow pages and looks up "Computers – Sales and Service." One ad catches his eye: "A-1 USED COMPUTERS – THEY'RE OLD... BUT THEY GET THE JOB DONE!" He notes down the address – and then – realizes with a groan – how the heck is he gonna get it home?! He phones the store, explains that he has the money to buy a computer but no car; will they deliver? Why, certainly they will, a creepy-sounding voice says. What kind of computer would he like?

Sheesh! He hadn't really thought about it. He knows $200 won't be enough for a modern type like they have at school... He glances around, eyes catching on the phone book ad, and says he just wants one that "can get the job done"... He needs it for schoolwork, he adds. No problem, they have just the thing; it's a bit of an antique, but it should serve him well. It's $199, including printer, and even sales tax! Okay, says Mark, I need it right away!

Soon the computer arrives. Mark's father (40s), Mr. Tyler, sees and wonders what's up; Mark says it's on "loan" to him from a friend; his father grunts and shuffles off. Mark takes the boxes into his room and rips them open. Gosh, it sure looks old, almost like an antique. The ones at school are sleek-looking; this one looks like – like something from somebody's attic!

Mark gets the computer up and running. What a great store, they even supplied paper for the printer! He clusters his history books and notes around him, sighs happily, and begins to type.

After a while, Mark's dad calls him for supper. Mark "saves" his work – he's finished several screens full of typing by now – pats the keyboard, and leaves the room. We close in on the computer screen. The screen, which has been emitting an eerie greenish glow, starts to glow even more strongly. Whirring and humming noises. Then a *very* strange thing happens. First, all the text gets "selected" ... then, every single letter instantly turns into an "x." The screen is suddenly, unaccountably, a solid block of x's!!

Poor unsuspecting Mark returns to his room and turns on the light. Looks at the screen: horror!! All his work is gone! Much fiddling with keys, but no change: those x's refuse to disappear. The screen is "frozen." Finally, as a last resort, he turns the computer off and back on again.

Immediately the screen full of x's returns, mocking him. This is unheard of! Panicky, Mark grabs the phone book, scrambles for that ad, and dials the phone number. No answer.

Mark bangs down the phone. He looks at his school calendar and counts off the days to his assignment deadline. Only two more days! Mark leaves the x's on the screen... maybe they'll be gone by morning... He'll call first thing tomorrow, and maybe the man in the store will help him.

He'd *better*.

The next morning, Mark is haggard from restless sleep and an overdose of worry. He gives the old heap of a computer a dirty look, then does an alarmed double-take. The x's are indeed gone! But in their place is this message:

TRUST ME

Mark slowly backs away, shaking his head in disbelief.

He frantically calls the used-computer store, but still no answer. He rips the store's ad out of the phone book and stuffs it in his school bag. His dad, on his third coffee, asks him if everything's all right, he looks kind of sick... Mark replies, with Oscar-performance brightness, that all is *fine*, dad! ...and off to school he goes, looking *very* sick indeed.

School is a blur: only history class stands out for Mark, and then, because it's such a drag. The teacher gleefully reminds everyone of their deadline two days away. Everyone groans, except Kenny, who's already handed in his paper, and Mark, who feels totally doomed.

At lunchtime, Mark and Kenny enter the cafeteria. Mark suddenly tells Kenny he'll be back in a few minutes; he turns around and heads for the payphone near the school office. Desperately he dials the computer-store number. Finally, that creepy voice answers. Mark tells the man about the x's wiping out his work. The man tells Mark that the computer must have a virus; it can easily be eliminated by putting in a floppy disk that has a special "disinfectant" on it. Great, says Mark at his sardonic worst. The man says Mark can come and pick it up after school. Free. I should *hope* it's free, says Mark!! Considering your "free" virus!!

After school, Mark leaves Kenny at the corner and says he has to do an errand for his dad. Paranoid now, making sure no classmate sees him, Mark gets on a bus and travels to the computer store. This is a very weird place – squeaky door, odd chimes, one lightbulb, owner (the creepy phone voice) who looks like he slept in mothballs, and used computers of all shapes and sizes.

The owner gives Mark the "disinfectant" disk, and tells him not to worry, didn't he believe the store's motto, "THEY'RE OLD... BUT THEY GET THE JOB DONE!"? Yeah but... Mark starts to complain, but the owner's beady black eyes bore into his head as he points a bony finger at the door, and tells him imperiously to go home. Mark eagerly complies; this guy scares the hell out of him.

Back at home: Mark dodges his

dad, says he has to work on his paper... Mr. Tyler says he's glad to see Mark finally settling down to schoolwork in a serious way. Mark goes to his room and warily peeks in the door, wondering what ominous words will appear on the screen of their own accord *this* time. But no, the words "***TRUST ME***" are still there. Mark shoves the "disinfectant" disk into the floppy drive.

Whirring and faint rumbling. Suddenly the "***TRUST ME***" message winks out and is replaced by the command:

SLEEP

As Mark stares at this new message, he indeed begins to feel sleepy, his eyes blink faster, he can't keep them open, he begins to slump in his chair; he just makes it over to his bed, and conks out, one foot dangling off the edge.

And now the computer goes to work. Keys are pressed by an unseen hand... slowly, one by one at first, then gradually gathering speed, until, while Mark enjoys the longest, most refreshing nap he ever had since he was a toddler, the keyboard softly chatters away... Word upon word, sentence upon sentence, paragraph upon paragraph, build on the screen and endlessly scroll and scroll....

Knocking at Mark's door. He is still fast asleep. The room is dead silent. Mr. Tyler calls his son's name, saying supper is ready. Mark begins to stir. Finally, his eyes pop open as he remembers... Mark tells his dad he'll be there in a minute; then he goes over to the computer. Mark is astounded at what he sees. On the computer screen are the words:

YOU'RE WELCOME

Reams of computer paper spill from the printer and down onto the floor. Mark grabs the paper and glances over it. It's a history essay... and there's his name at the top right, his teacher's name and classroom number at top left... and it looks – gulp! – *perfect*!

<u>End of Act One</u>

<u>Act Two</u>

Mark and Kenny are back at the tennis court. Kenny says he was glad to see that Mark was able to finish his history assignment so fast, and even hand it in a day early! Mark just smiles and says cryptically that he must have been "inspired." Kenny says that the computer must have been a great help. Mark says, "More than you'll ever know."

It's a few days later. History class. Mark's teacher is calling out students' names and handing back their history papers. Kenny has earned an "A" and pumps his fist, grinning at Mark. All the papers are given out this way, and Mark's name still hasn't been called. He's kind of anxious by now. Finally, the teacher stares at Mark and says he wants to see him after class. Mark is definitely feeling uncomfortable...

Mark sits facing the teacher, who's sitting at his desk. He is holding Mark's paper. This paper, he says, is excellent. This is an A+ paper, he says. Mark holds his breath. The only little problem he says, is that it's not yours. Mark is stricken, but just manages to stammer "not... n-not mine? uh... what – what do you mean?" The teacher tells Mark that the essay is virtually an exact replica of a chapter in a book which he, the teacher, just happens to own. Mark looks mortified. The teacher goes on, saying that such a transgression is called "plagiarism" and is unacceptable. Mark is to receive an

"F" grade on the paper *and* on the entire course, unless he writes a "make-up" paper, *original* this time, and twice as long.

A defeated, disappointed and angry Mark arrives home after school. The computer tricked him! Mark goes to his room, and approaches the computer, in a rage. You stupid, mean – he starts to yell at it... but then he gets close and reads the taunting two-line message on its screen. It says:

***FROM ONE THIEF TO ANOTHER! ***

***WHO YOU GONNA TELL? ***

Arghhhhh! Mark punches his fists down on the keyboard. The message "***TEMPER, TEMPER! ***" appears under the two lines already there, mocking him even more. Mark flips out. He scours the room and grabs the handiest hard object he can find, a baseball bat propped in a corner. In slow-motion rage Mark swings the bat at the screen with all his might, SMASHING it to smithereens on contact. Sparks and glass slivers go flying everywhere; luckily, he'd squeezed his eyes shut for the hit. The computer is now an ex-computer, a pile of rubble spewing foul neon-greenish smoke.

Mr. Tyler is on the scene at once, waving away the smoke, spluttering, demanding to know what the hell has happened. A very resigned and exhausted Mark knows: the jig is up. I gotta talk to you, Dad, says Mark, and father and son go down the hall to the kitchen...where Mark, we assume, spills his whole story.

Mr. Tyler, grim-faced, ad in hand, begins to place a call to A-1 USED COMPUTERS, as a repentant Mark, back in his room, searches his drawer for that cursed black wallet he found. He grasps it and brings it to his dad just as he is hanging up, shaking his head. No answer at the store.

Mr. Tyler orders him to return the wallet to its owner – a Ms. A. Seaton – immediately, and tells him he must offer to repay the stolen money with work, chores, anything he can do for her. No, he will *not* go with Mark; he got himself into this mess all by himself, now he has to get himself *out* of it alone, too.

Mark on the bus, heading to this Ms. Seaton's place. The bus is empty and silent; Mark looks very lonely and pitiful hunched in his seat, head bowed, a picture of contrition.

The driver tells Mark they've reached the right street, and lets him off. Mark gets out and looks around. This place is in the boonies. He finds the address, walks up the path between well-manicured lawns to the front door, and knocks. Pleasant-looking Ms. Seaton (40s) answers the door.

Mark explains that he found her wallet a few days ago...there *was* money in it, but... could he come in and explain...? Ms. Seaton invites him in.

Ms. Seaton is very friendly, bubbly, and grateful for her wallet's return. She doesn't seem too concerned about the missing money, oddly enough. But when Mark offers his "services" as restitution, and begs her to assign him some sort of work he can do, she begins to ponder... Wel-l-l, perhaps there *is* something... Tell me, she asks, are you a fast typist? Oh yes, he assures her, he always got best marks in typing; he's been typing for many years cause his handwriting is so lousy. Well, Ms. Seaton says, I think I have just the job for you! Tell you what, it's late now, tomorrow's Saturday, would you like to start in the morning? Say, 9:00 sharp? I'll prepare all the instructions for you. Mark winces at the early "call time" but has to agree that he'll return. She notes down his name and phone number and address, just in case.

Mark returns home. Tells his father what happened, and Mr. Tyler grunts in assent. Mark passes a fitful night.

Saturday morning, the unforgiving alarm clock awakens Mark. He glances to the empty spot on his desk where the malevolent antique computer had sat, and groans... Last night's glass carnage has been cleaned up... but he could swear he still sees a very faint greenish glow hovering over the desk...

Mark: back on the bus, not so alone now, but still hunched and pathetic. He arrives again at Ms. Seaton's house; she greets him warmly.

Come with me, I've got everything ready for you, she says. Mark follows Ms. Seaton down the hall. This is a cheerfully decorated house, bright colours, very upbeat. A contrast to Mark's house, which has been kind of sombre and neglected since his mother's death.

They reach Ms. Seaton's study. She gestures toward a table heaped with stacks of books and periodicals. Ms. Seaton explains that she's a history professor working on a book, and there is much data to be entered. I've made up a list of instructions for you, she tells him, it's right on the desk. Oh, you *do* know how to use a computer, I hope? I have such a habit of assuming things, she says. Mark assures her that he is indeed computer-literate. Uh, where, he asks her, where *is* your computer? Oh, it's just under the flowered cloth there; I don't like things to get dusty. Well, go to it, she chirps, as she turns and leaves the room.

Mark goes to the flower-printed cloth which covers a hulking shape, and strips it off. Arghhhhh!! There sits a perfect replica – no doubt about it – of the maniacal computer he thought he had "killed" yesterday! Mark's jaw drops in horror. Suddenly he hears a loud "click" behind him; he whirls around to see that the door has closed. He goes to it, tries the handle, it's locked! Rattles it, bangs on the door, nothing happens. Hey, he yells. Bangs on door. No sound.... except... a faint whirring, rumbling noise, inside the room. He slowly, very slowly, turns to look, and sees – the eerie glowing screen of the computer, with a message on it.... in fact, it's a poem, and it says:

ZERO, ONE, TWO, THREE

CAN YOU TYPE AS FAST AS ME?

Back to campfire setting – wind-up: Mark finished the school year okay, except for two subjects: history and computers. Somehow, he lost his taste for them.

The End

An aside: I've just noticed, digging in my computer folder of script files, in one of its sub-folders, that my *Antique Computer* story wasn't my only screenplay idea back then. In fact, the folder is a veritable treasure trove of notes, half-finished, which I'd all but forgotten. Maybe one day I'll actually finish one of them!

****

I worked on *Are You Afraid of the Dark* for three seasons, and did many other shows in between. Finally, I had to stop being *"Afraid"* since the other contracts were taking over, and were just too tempting to turn down.

PART THREE – ALLEGRO FILMS

Between 1994 and 1999 I worked on over a dozen films at Allegro. This was a great company for someone like me, working on contract. In truth, the whole business was perfect: I would have a TV series for several months, then get unemployment insurance (euphemistically called employment insurance by the "government gods" here) until my next contract. Many of those gigs were at Allegro. I worked on those shows on site, since almost all of them were on PCs, and I was still a Mac girl at home. My family and I have always been "Mac evangelists," what can I tell you!

Most of the shows I worked on there were MOWs (Movies of the Week), with '80s stars like Molly Ringwald, say, or Nancy McKeon. But my first big Allegro show was a feature film slated for theatrical release.

Screamers: No, I am not a script "typist"!

Screamers, based on a story by much-lauded science-fiction writer Philip K. Dick (*Blade Runner, Minority Report* and much more), appealed to the sci-fi fan in me. It was about some humans and these bad little robots that, well, screamed. There was blood… not the robots'.

Working on site this time meant that I

commuted every day to the eastern edge of downtown Montreal, in the lower-Plateau area. The company comprised an entire huge building. Production offices usually occupied large-enough premises to accommodate all departments or at least the coordinators of all of them.

On *Screamers,* rather than being placed downstairs in the production offices, I was ensconced in a little room upstairs, just down the hall from the office of Tom Berry, the founder and president of the company. He settled me at a computer and brought up the file. There it was in all its gory glory, in the Word formatting I was accustomed to seeing.

I should mention that thanks to this company, I had the privilege of seeing my first emails ever. Well, I didn't actually see the emails per se. Nor did I know they were called emails! But there I was, formatting *Screamers* script revisions, when all of a sudden, a small rectangular window just popped up on my screen, emitting a little beep, startling the heck out of me, announcing YOU HAVE MAIL!

It seems that Allegro had had an "intranet" mail system installed for their employees, and darned if I'd ever seen that before. Huh, modern technology, eh? 1994. My heart is all a-flutter with nostalgia.

My only bone to pick with Allegro regarding *Screamers* is the credit they ended up giving me on it. What can I say? Credits matter to us lowly film slaves. Well the money is good so we weren't slaves – I take that back – but: credits! We *lust* for credits. But not just any credit. No, it must reflect our hard-earned efforts and take into account our lofty station (if any) on the production. In the absence of a lofty station, if we could at least get an accurate credit, that would be nice.

On Screamers I entered script revisions, did formatting, did proofreading and even light editing of errors I found. Tom certainly seemed appreciative of this last bit. What I did *not* do, is just type. A *child* can type. Yet the credit they gave me at the end of the film was "Script Typist." I have one very erudite thing to say to that: Booooo!

Of all the gigs I had in the film biz, that was the only one to give me such a lowly credit. On some shows, I was called a "script revisor." (Still better than just "typist"!) On others: "script coordinator." Oh well. Nowhere to go but up after that! And that is where I went. Except for this next thing.

The software from hell

Due to the tedium of manual script formatting in Word, it was only a matter of time before inventors came up with software dedicated to the job of automatically doing all the formatting for you. Allegro got their hands on this software, which was cleverly called "Scriptor." And I had to use it in my next gig there, after *Screamers*.

"Scriptor" was the bane of my existence. It almost made me quit the work that I had come to love. The first time I used it, I was toiling for one of the Allegro production managers on staff, Renaud Mathieu, a terrific guy. The script was *The Paper Boy*. (Not the one with Nicole Kidman – this was a different film.)

At first I was excited because it meant working on a Mac this time. Oh joy, I thought, I'll feel right at home!

No! I did not feel at home at all! In fact, I felt like I'd died and gone to a very nasty corner of hell! Okay, so the software program called Scriptor must've seemed promising, and must've worked fine – in sterile laboratory conditions.

But *not* in the real world of script changes on top of changes on top of changes. At least, not for me.

The biggest problem, I found, was that it was so totally unforgiving. By that, I mean that if you locked the pages but then found that you'd made one tiny mistake, you had to go back to the beginning and do everything ALL OVER. I'm talking hours of wasted work, just because the program didn't take into account that 1) humans are fallible, and 2) you sometimes just need to do ONE LITTLE THING over. Not the whole darn mess.

Renaud, having tried out the program before, was nice enough to help me figure out how to circumvent its crazy, un-user-friendly tendencies and *make* things work, almost in spite of it. If you're reading this, Renaud, *merci mille fois*!

After *Paper Boy*, I never had to use Scriptor again… at Allegro, that is. I did have to use it on a couple of other gigs – unfortunately. I still didn't understand the program perfectly, and didn't have Renaud around to help me! I'll get to one of those other shows later on; it merits its own section. (I use the term "merit" loosely.)

After my miserable experiences with Scriptor, you can't fault me for being hesitant whenever newer software programs became available a couple of years later. But once I learned them, they were amazing and saved so much time!

A note about working conditions

By the mid-1990s, as my name gradually became known in Hollywood North circles as someone capable of doing script revisions, I started to get many calls. Amazingly, I was able to juggle almost all the shows, rarely having to say no. (Don't ever say no!) I started to build a coterie of people as liaisons who would call upon me whenever they themselves got work on a show, usually as production managers, production coordinators or first ADs. I would see the same people and teams of people over and over, which made for great camaraderie. It was like getting to see good friends again or, at least, friendly faces. So, it was usually a very amiable milieu in which to work.

I never knew how long each gig would last. A TV series or mini-series could be good for several months. But a one-off feature film would more often be a matter of weeks. I would start during the pre-production period, when all the aspects of filmmaking, such as casting, set design and construction, costumes and so on, were in the preparation phase, before shooting. During the shoot, I was still needed to process script revisions as they went along. Some shows required me more often than others, and for a longer period, so I would always be on call.

Sometimes I worked at home, sometimes on site, as I've mentioned. Working on site meant I soon learned a lot about my city, and drove to many areas I'd never been in before, which made things interesting. It tested my sense of direction, since this was all pre-GPS!

When I worked from home, an office driver (or other crew person, and sometimes even a producer) would bring a hard copy of a script to me. After I was done, my script revisions were usually printed out and then picked up by a driver who took them to the production office to be photocopied and distributed. Later on, email came into play.

Occasionally I was lucky enough when working on site to have my own office. Often, I shared one. And sometimes I was stuck in a hallway! Good thing I learned to have a laser-like focus. (My occasional tunnel vision, which maybe wasn't such a good thing in other areas of my life, now came in handy!)

A glitch in time...

After *Screamers* I moved into the huge space downstairs at Allegro to work, and was given a cross between a cubicle and a walk-in closet. Hey, it had walls! Walls were good! Anyway, sometime after *The Paper Boy* debacle on Scriptor, by the mid-'90s, we transitioned to a way better program for script revisions, called Final Draft. At last we had software that worked like it was supposed to! Its creators fully understood what was needed and useful, and put it all in. (It is still in use today, 20 years later, confirming its efficacy.) Now I was off to the races, working on one MOW after another, and enjoying myself immensely.

But one fine day...

FADE IN: I was inputting some script changes that one of the producers was giving me verbally, pacing back and forth behind me. This would always make me nervous; I would imagine the person looking over my shoulder, just waiting for a mistake so he could pounce. After we'd been going through the changes for about 40 minutes or so, he dictating to me as I typed, one line he said didn't make sense.

"Um... wait," I said, uncertainly, butterflies instantly fluttering in my stomach. "Wait, what did you say? That's not what I have here," I said, pointing to my screen. "Here it says: 'She walks out of the room slowly, sobbing while – '"

"What?!" he yelled. "That's not right! The scene should end *there*, and then she..."

FADE OUT, mercifully.

It turned out that I was working from the wrong version. A MAJOR MISTAKE. It seems that when I was given the diskette, no one thought to point out to me which was the most recent script version that had been worked on. (Another person had fiddled with this script before me; it was still in a preliminary stage.) But I should have *asked.* So I was working on an older version, prior to the hard copy that the now-irate producer was holding in his hands.

We'd just wasted a lot of time, and this first-time producer, who apparently was nervous him*self*, was none too pleased. But I learned an important lesson – to check and re-check multiple times which version I should be working on.

And *he* learned not to work with me again. Can't win 'em all, right?

****

The last show I worked on at Allegro bookended my history with them – it was another sci-fi film called *Xchange* – featuring creepy clones – and starring the innocuous Stephen Baldwin. I didn't get a credit on this one, as I was just helping out by subbing for the director's assistant, who was also doing the script revisions. At one point, she wasn't available, so they quickly whisked me in to do the changes, *stat* – and then I was whisked back out.

Working at Allegro on many projects over several years gave me the opportunity to fine-tune my skills as well as to meet innumerable players in the business, who later hired me on other shows after Allegro Films was no more. I have nothing but appreciation for the company Tom Berry founded that fed many mouths of cast and crew in Montreal's burgeoning film biz 20 years ago. Without them, we all might have had to pull in our belts a little tighter.

Speaking of belt-tightening, I sure wish I'd been able to turn a blind eye to all those carbohydrate-laden goodies in the company's kitchen...

PART FOUR – KIDS IN ORBIT

In 1995 I started working on the first season of *Space Cases,* a funny and clever sci-fi series for kids – kind of like *Star Trek* meets Nickelodeon. Which makes sense, since it was co-produced by Nickelodeon in the U.S. and by Cinar, a major player on the Montreal film scene at the time. (Too bad scandal and financial chicanery led to Cinar's implosion a few years later.) The Season One production office was located in a true hipster area of Montreal: hardwood floors, high ceilings, reclaimed woodwork galore.

The trouble with David

I got along famously with the executive story consultant, David Gerrold, who came with a storied past in the TV-sci-fi world. He was especially noted for having written the most famous episode for the original 1967 *Star Trek,* "The Trouble with Tribbles," about the over-breeding puff-ball aliens taken aboard the Enterprise (a decision later greatly regretted by the Enterprise crew, particularly Captain Kirk). The episode was an apt metaphor for how little things can sometimes overtake and haunt us.

What I remember most about David, though, is the fact that he told me he was going to produce a new hour-long sci-fi series to be called "Space Wolf" (no relation to *Space*

Cases), and he wanted to do it in Montreal – *and* he wanted me to be script coordinator on it. Music to my ears, right? Since he worked on a PC, he asked me to start researching new Windows-based script-processing software available that we could both utilize on his new show. I researched like crazy and came up with several choices on the Internet's nascent World Wide Web. I then sent him a detailed memo when he was back in L.A., explaining the results of my research:

MEMO

To: David Gerrold
From: Ellie Presner
Re Space Wolf - script software
Date: Jan. 20/96

Hi there in sunny LA from frigid Mtl.!

Here's what I found so far re script formatting software available for Windows:

Script Wizard for WinWord 2.0/6.0
        $US 175.00
Side By Side for WinWord
        price??
ScriptRighter for WinWord 6.0
        $CAD 99.00
ScriptWright for Winword 6.0/7.0
        $US 99.00

ScriptWright is a sophisticated program which runs in Word 6.0.

ScriptWright 6.1b on the PC is

guaranteed to run (16-bit) Word 6 on Windows 3.x, Windows 95, and Windows NT, and will soon be available for Word 7.0 32-bit (Office 95 for Windows 95). It is written by Guy Gallo (of GScript fame) and Geoffrey Teabo of Indelible Ink. I particularly like the way the program offers the tools of a stand-alone screenwriting package, yet manages to squeeze every ounce of value out of Word's already vast existing features. Indelible Ink was kind enough to send me a copy of ScriptWright to try out, hence the free plug.

There is also a program called "Script Thing" which so far has been for DOS only, but they're soon supposedly coming out with a Windows version. Meanwhile they sent me manual & demo of the DOS version.

So what's new re the show??

Talk to you soon...

Ellie

****

And he never replied. That was when I first heard of the expression, "vapourware."[3]

David Gerrold wasn't with us for the second season. Creative differences, it was rumoured.

---

[3] Originally pertaining to software, but later expanded to refer to anything promised but never actually happening.

The launch of Season Two

When Season Two of *Space Cases* started in the summer of 1996, our offices moved to Mel's Cité du Cinema, new home of Cinar's productions; this was *the* cutting-edge Montreal studio in the '90s. Every big feature or series aspired to shoot there, as everything of top-notch quality was in one convenient place: production facilities, offices and sound stage. Located on Île du Havre, right next to the iconic Jacques Cartier Bridge, it was nestled in quite a picturesque setting, which – weather permitting – meant you could enjoy a pleasant picnic lunch outside by the St. Lawrence River.

By the time we began Season 2, I was feeling way more comfortable with – well, with everything! I understood more about the roles of various crew, my own role (and excellent new software), just the entire amazing collaborative process of filmmaking. I was able to relax and have great fun with my work and with my friendly, accommodating colleagues on this gig.

The script process fascinated me more than ever before. I found myself sitting in on many meetings and taking copious notes. I felt more… *invested* in the show. It was probably due to working on site for many months, with the same people over two seasons of prep and shooting.

The creators and co-writers of the show, Bill Mumy *(Lost in Space, Babylon 5)* and Peter David (*Babylon 5, Oblivion*), were a couple of truly original and funny guys who had cut their teeth on a frothy mix of science fiction and pop culture, both of which were blended into the fun-fest that was *Space Cases.*

The story was about a small group of kids, would-be space explorers from some future "Starcademy," who are marooned on a spaceship, the Christa (named in tribute to the late space-shuttle Challenger astronaut, Christa McAuliffe) – along with their humourless teeth-gritting commander and teacher, the only adults on the ship. Oh, plus a clumsy female android named Thelma – goofily played by the talented Montreal-born actress, Anik Matern. There was also a cute little robot called Gizbot, a bit of a ripoff of R2D2, since he (it was assumed to be male) was small, rolled around and didn't speak.

Peter – originally a comic-book writer/creator – loved incorporating in-jokes, pop-culture references, puns and other wordplay in his episodes. Some of Peter's episode names were "King of the Hil" (The Hil were a race of aliens); "A Star is Boring"; "Prisoner of Luff"; and "Breath of a Salesman." The stalwart hero's name was Harlan – a shout-out to one of Peter's favourite authors, Harlan Ellison. Many of the first season's episodes were named after famous songs, like "Both Sides Now" and "Nowhere Man." Peter's love of wordplay and in-jokes made the show extremely parent-friendly. The whole family could enjoy watching them, albeit on different levels.

Another important figure around the office was Ted Jessup, who was Nickelodeon's main man on the ground with the title of "executive in charge of production." I think he earned his pay, since many little – or big – fires found their way to Ted's desk for him to put out.

It's funny, the odd little things that stick with you. I recall one production meeting, held as usual in Ted's office, with the overflow of people (not enough chairs!) sitting on the floor, hippie-style. (As somewhat of an ex-hippie myself, I was used to that.) There was some script change or other being discussed, and he asked me, across the room, "You have that, Ellie?"

I squinted at my marked-up pages, searching frantically for the new note, as all eyes in the room were on me. "Uhh…"

He pointed to someone else, an art-department person involved in this change, and then pointed to me, back and forth, saying, "You. And you. Interface."

It was the most succinct bit of direction I have ever heard from a producer. Ted was efficient, in my view. He went on to good things, writing for *The Late Late Show with Craig Kilborn,* as well as most recently writing and producing for *Family Guy.*

Valri

I think the main reason I loved working on *Space Cases* so much had a lot to do with my sharing a tiny closet – I mean office – with the amazingly funny and down-to-earth Valri Bromfield. Val faced her computer at one wall and I faced the opposite one; our seat backs were practically touching, that's how close we were.

Valri was an alumna of *SCTV Channel*, *Kids in the Hall, Grace Under Fire* and The *David Letterman Show, and* was a writer and gifted comic actress. (After *Space Cases,* she would go on to be a staff writer on *The Rosie O'Donnell Show.)* She'd had over 20 years' experience with story and comedy, and the *Space Cases* execs were lucky to land her as story editor and writer. She could have behaved like a diva with me, yet she was anything but.

Hoo boy, did we make each other laugh. And sometimes we cried. Or laughed to keep from crying. Or laughed *and* cried at the same time. Script changes every five minutes will do that to you.

We fuelled each other's crazy humour. One day, giddy from the long hours and endless rewrites I had to process, I wrote a short scene myself and nonchalantly passed the printout behind me to Val. I waited for her to erupt. It didn't take long. This is exactly what I wrote:

```
25B  EXT.  CHRISTA  ENCAMPMENT  -
NIGHT  -  RADU,  SUZEE,  ROSIE,
THELMA, GIZBOT

They've got their backpacks on
and are rushing to the rescue.
```

```
Just  before  they  exit  frame,
Rosie turns back to the Christa.
The Gizbot is motoring around a
moment,  and  then  he  moves  off
camera. As  he  motors  off,  his
shiny  metallic  testicles  bump
along,  emitting  sparks  as  they
hit   every   pebble   in   sight,
thereby  starting  a  huge  forest
fire  in  which  the  Christa  is
totally  demolished  and  all  the
Space  Cases  are  killed...except
Rosie,  who,  true  to  character,
is heat-impervious.
```

Val howled with glee. (It was commonly known that Val was gay, so this gave my little scene an extra soupçon of mischief.)

****

Just to give you an idea of the kinds of script- and story-meeting notes we often dealt with: here's an excerpt of some notes I took at a meeting between Val and Ted, on one of the episodes. I put the notes into a memo to Peter. They would help guide his rewrites.

Hi Peter!

Notes from meeting of Ted & Val:

Note changed jeopardy. (Ted says it must come from "outside.") Once Davenport changes the molecular structure of everyone, because of her head, they are preoccupied as in Act One existing script. BUT while their attention is taken off the ship, it wanders off course and is heading toward certain destruction (e.g. into a sun). This realization should be END OF ACT ONE break.

Act Two:

The characters attempt to work with their switched personalities, to save themselves. Re scene in the command Post: Radu tries to be the leader that Harlan is, but he can't pull it off – he's truly a support man. Harlan tries to separate his thoughts from the sounds in his head that keep him from being the supportive person his post requires. Bova and Rosie, inside each other, are just useless to the ship's safety. (…)

Please note: Ted dictated changes in Teaser and First Act, and Act Two up to page 19, where we hit a wall.

****

See that? I love that they admitted they "hit a wall." Seriously. On many shows I worked on, you'd never get an exec and a story editor to confess that to a writer!

Of course, a few days later, the notes may have changed yet again, and there'd certainly be additional ones. No wonder Val and I were both kept very busy! (Mind you, until I worked on *The Hunger*, I didn't really know the meaning of *busy*.)

And here are a few notes from Val on Season 2's Runaway:

> Overconfidence – Play this out. Who was overconfident?
> In the Starling make Harlan do something rash. Put him in the Starling.
> ACT ONE
> All action – no character.
> Needs some meat.
> Harlan basically shoots and drives.
> Maybe a show-off. Teaser in which the guys are playing at being Stardogs
> – imitations – but Bova gets carried away – the little one being included.
> PUT HARLAN IN THE STARLING!
> Implications?
> Act One, Scene 7: The runaway ship should be under control by now?
> ACT TWO
> The jump tube stuff is a runner not a story.

Two much techno talk – lots of action – not enough character story.
Tractor Beam?? What's that?

＊＊＊＊

You might say Val was like a – well, like a Script Cop, keeping the writers honest, making them stick to the bible (the "rules" and details of the show's "universe" which must be adhered to). Her job also involved adding punch and jokes wherever they were deemed to be lacking.

Script dizziness

My role as script coordinator included the inputting of all the changes which showered down on me every day, keeping all the different versions straight, and all the *episodes* straight – since more than one episode was always in some stage of preparation or production. Along the way, of course, I had to keep the formatting correct and uniform, page numbers and scene numbers accurate, "massaging" or tweaking pages when necessary to keep the proper pagination.

If you had looked in my *Space Cases* script folder on my computer at the time, you would have seen a sub-folder for each episode. Let's call the first episode Sillyscript. This script is now at the stage of pink page revisions, so I would have the file called Sillyscript.pink in the folder. But in the same big Sillyscript folder, I would also have all previous versions, like Sillyscript.white, Sillyscript.proddraft, and even Sillyscript.outline, Sillyscript.logline, etc. (A logline is a succinct description of a show, usually one sentence. I got good at writing them on my next series, *The Hunger*.) All this, in case some someone needed to look back and see what we used to have in Act III Scene 4C, in the production draft. Of course, that same someone now wants to reinstate part of it into the pink. So now it will be a *blue* revision. Piece of cake, right?

Meanwhile, also lurking in my *Space Cases* script folder, episode two is already up to its green revisions, and that file would be called Greatscript.green. Again, all the previous versions would still be in that script's folder as well, with their different names, like Greatscript.blue, Greatscript.pink, and so on. Just in case! I got so used to keeping everything, that to this day, I still have the most recent coloured revision in my computer of all the episodes. (Unfortunately, I can't open them – I no longer have Final Draft software!)

To further enhance your glimpse of what it was like juggling all the changes, here's a wacky email I sent to Val when she'd gone for a quick visit home (on the West Coast):

Aug. 23/96 – e-mail to Valri

Hiya, Val. Hope you had a good trip home!

Not much new around these parts. I should mention that that cute lil Hil Shaman and I had a little baby Hil; we named it "Mound"... So far, not too much jealousy from its half-siblings, Mockingbird and Blueberry.

Ted decided to have his nephew, Lemuel, age 10, do a punch-up of Motherlode... he punched it so well it got knocked out by page 22...

Oh, sorry to tell you, Margie decided to kill Homeward Bound.

Insufficient kid issue, she said. But it's ok, a new script was submitted by Nick's new wonderboys, Beavis & Butthead. Only problem is, it's only 15 pages long. Filled with "eh-eh-ehs"... But that's ok. Peter will supplement it with a tad more dialogue and sci-fi stuff... then it'll be 42 pages.

The rest of the scripts are in fine shape, ready to roll. Except that Nick has decided that the order of shooting will be completely reversed. Also, our work schedule has been changed to Wednesday-to-Sunday...except for weeks of the new moon, when it will be Thursday p.m. to the following Tuesday right after lunch...IF it's the good caterer. But no work on Thanksgiving. We'll all be going up to Anik's country place for a turkey shoot/orgy.

Irene has decided to leave for Hollywood where she will star in a feature about l'Oréal products.

Adam is moving to Key West to open a specialized fax/photocopy service, to be called "Scripts-R-Us"...

Wait! I almost forgot! The premise of the much-maligned Both Sides Now has been totally changed. Rosie finds a Magic Ring in the Christa's hitherto-undiscovered glove compartment. (Originally, the Ring had a label saying, "Eat Me," but Nick vetoed that...)

The Space Cases soon discover that whoever puts on the Ring takes on, temporarily, the powers of Albie Hecht. Sadly, no one wants to wear the Ring for very long. There is hot debate over whether the episode title should be Ring-Around-A- Rosie, or Lords of the Ring...

Well, in closing, Val, you can see that you haven't missed much... I mean, just another typical coupla days at Space Cases Productions, right? Oh, gotta go, I have to do doublegold revisions on Truth Hurts. Take care, and see you Monday!

Love, Ellie

****

And here's a short excerpt of a memo I sent to Val a few weeks later, as we were nearing the end of Season 2's script preparation.

Sept. 26/1996

Hi Val! Keepin' u informed!

BOTH SIDES NOW –
Blue revisions being agonized over even as I type –
Sept. 26

RUNAWAY –
Pink changes done Sept. 20.

MOTHERLODE –
Table draft done Sept. 20. – faxed to Billy Kimball (of New Line) for humour punch – Sept. 24.

TROUBLE WITH DOUBLES –
Rev. 3rd draft done Sept. 5 (small distribution).

A FRIEND IN NEED –
2nd draft done WED. Sept. 4.

****

Me again. It's a wonder we didn't get dizzy! Well, maybe we did, a little.

An incubator

Summer melted into fall, and the show began to wind down. It had been a fantastic learning experience for me, and fun, too!

I think of those two seasons as a kind of incubator of talent, for the cast, yes, but also – especially – for the directors. Some of the directors who worked on *Space Cases* were in the early stages of their careers, which began to really take off afterwards.

A perfect example is Vincenzo Natali, who directed his first-ever show, an episode of *Space Cases* in Season 2. He has since written and directed the cult sci-fi hits *Cube* and *Splice*, and directed many other films and TV series – episodes of *Earth: Final Conflict, Darknet, Ascension, The Returned, Orphan Black and Hannibal*. The list goes on; Vince has become the go-to guy for eerie stories.

Then there's Stephen Williams. After his episode of *Space Cases,* Stephen helmed episodes of – to name only some – *Psi Factor: Chronicles of the Paranormal, Blue Murder, Dark Angel, Lost, Prime Suspect, Person of Interest, How To Get Away With Murder, The Walking Dead…* and tons more. We can see that Stephen was also more than a little attracted to the dark side.

Adam Weissman went in another direction, specializing in children's shows. One look at his filmography on the IMDb shows you he has been a super-busy bee. Same goes for

John Bell and David Straiton. Iain Paterson, who had directed episodes of *Space Cases* and *Are You Afraid of the Dark* went on to produce scores of shows, including the illustrious *House of Cards.*

And what of my pal Val? As I mentioned earlier, she moved on to *The Rosie O'Donnell Show.* As often happens in this business, I lost touch with her; I moved on as well. But not before sending her one last email, letting her know what she missed at the *Space Cases* wrap party. She'd had to leave before the party took place. It gives you a good idea of how people let their hair down after working their butts off for so long. Also, at the end, it indicates how – for me at least – it had reached the point where one gig was starting to lead right into another.

It's a wrap!

Date: Mon. Nov. 4, 1996
To: Val
From Ellie Presner
Subject: The Wrap Party!

Hiya Val!

OK, picture this:

Studio D all dolled up, party-like. 2 real live casino tables brought in, roulette & blackjack, wi. pretend money doled out to start... a raffle "pot" won *twice* by Nick people

– Adam & Ted – who gallantly dumped their prizes back in (to a chorus of "fixed! fixed!")

Music with a good thumpin' beat... Anik leading the bunny hop round the studio... speaking of which... Anik dressed to kill in long slinky black gown, hair up, blood-red lipstick... lil *Paige* in a long slinky gown, size minus-12...

Paige's mom, Monica, with cleavage down to there... I said to her "gee, ur even more daring than i am!" (as i pointed to my own modest deep V-neck), and she said, "distracts 'em from my stomach," pointing to her rounded tum. i love it... :-)

Ted: dancing. Please don't make me say more. OK. U twisted my arm. Can u dig it: *every single part of his body* bopping to the rhythm– or should I say rhythms – separately, each part with a mind of its own – I had to stare. I didn't think the human body could *do* that!!!!!

Peter, resplendent in off-white jacket... dancing with me, to "Hot! Hot! Hot!" Now HE can dance. Too bad he has to puff & pant for every desperate breath in my face while he's doing it, poor guy... <I'm *so* mean! <g>>

Kristian,[4] regaling me with his story ideas for next season...[5] ok, so I asked him...;->

Paul Boretski[6] looking adorable, giving me a bone-crushing hug (there were LOTS of hugs/kisses that night – I suspect the booze helped.<grin>)... as his ultra-perky C. Tiegs-lookalike wife sat nearby...

Free booze galore of course, & so-so canapes...

Adam, cool/laid-back as per usual, with ass't Gina in tow – finally, the face behind the fax!

Ted telling me I did a *great* job... :-D Heey, so the space cadet[7] *does* pay attention after all...heheheh

Anyhoo, wished u were there!!! We coulda giggled together!

On other fronts: so I now have TWO new shows, well three, if u count the feature ("Little

---

[4] Kristian Ayre played the co-lead character, "Radu."

[5] It turned out there *was* no "next season."

[6] He played Commander Goddard on the Christa spaceship.

[7] I only called him that because with his long hair and typical denim overalls he wore, he looked like a throwback hippie.

Men") I just worked on for past 2 weeks, and also will go in tomorrow for what I hope will be the last time, for yellow revisions! But get this: I got "The Hunger," a gothic/horror series for Showtime, *20* episodes!! It'll take me thru til April!!! Started today!

****

And now, before I get to the special roller coaster that was *The Hunger*, I must first tell you about a sublime interlude I experienced between the two seasons of *Space Cases*.

PART FIVE – THE PRISONER
A WILLING CAPTIVE

A Sunday in May. 9:55 a.m. The doorman ushers me through the gilded doors of Montreal's storied hotel jewel, the Ritz Carlton. Home of Elizabeth Taylor's first marriage ceremony with Richard Burton, 1964, and now: Ellie Presner and Patrick McGoohan's work on a *Prisoner* movie script, 1996!

I'm at the door to his suite. I knock, with as much confidence as I can muster.

The door opens.

Meeting "Number Six"

Whatever I was expecting, this isn't it. I had the image of his *Prisoner* character in my brain – silly, though, when you think about it – that was thirty years ago! Who has *not* changed in thirty years? He was almost 40 then, so now he's... 69.

First I see the white beard. Small, very neat. His hair is white. He smiles at me. He has on a silk smoking-jacket over clothes – it's a black and maroon print with black lapels. He opens the door and stands aside to let me in:

"Hello! Hello, Ellie!" he booms, grinning, blue eyes twinkling. "Pleasure to meet you!"

"Uh same *here,*" I stammer, and grin back. We shake hands. He has a solid grip.

Okay! I tell my nervous self: just be *me.*

My imperfect, goofy, irreverent, sometimes-downright-funny self. That does the trick, and I relax. Besides, I am, after all, carrying a laptop in a briefcase. (I once did a visualization exercise, back in the touchy-feely '70s, wherein I tried to picture my future self. I was just coming up for air after staying at home for a bunch of years, post-babies. Whatever my future self would be up to, she'd definitely be carrying a briefcase.)

He shows me into the suite's gracious living room, which is ginormous! My entire apartment that I lived in at the time could've easily fit into it.

This is way before the hotel closes for renovations in 2008, so it still retains a lot of its old-world filigreed and velvet glory. The room has (naturally!) a big fireplace, with what appear to be some of Patrick's family photos on the mantel.

There are many chairs that seem to be genuine antiques to me – non-expert that I am – and large important-looking paintings hang on the walls.

He shows me the huge bedroom and sumptuous bathroom.

He asks me if I'd like coffee or tea, and orders it from room service. Then we sit at two of these "antique" chairs and make small talk. We arrange my hourly pay to the satisfaction of us both: $25 per hour on weekdays; $50 per hour on weekends.

As I sip my coffee I try to steady my quivering hands.

The Prisoner Cult

Now relax, dear readers, I must digress for a moment to tell you – those of you who may not already know – about the cult TV show, *The Prisoner,* that Patrick McGoohan starred in back in 1967-68, for all of its 17 episodes. (For those already steeped in their knowledge of *Prisoner* lore, you may move on.)

In addition to lending his charismatic presence and sonorous voice to the show as the lead actor, he also co-created the thing in the first place along with David Tomblin, and contributed hugely to it as a writer, director and producer.

The Prisoner was filmed in England and Wales for the British television production company, ITV, and eventually made its way to TV screens around the world. I don't think anyone foresaw the magnitude of its effect on viewers, especially youth. Its stance was anti-authoritarian, even revolutionary. Its clarion call was the cry of Number Six – Patrick's character's name in the series: "I am not a number! I am a free man!" The show's surrealistic style was way ahead of its time, say its aficionados and critics alike.

The story was, in a nutshell: a secret agent who has suddenly quit gets kidnapped and brought to a strange island village, where he is held captive and tries many times (in increasingly creative ways) in vain to escape. Obviously, the show had great appeal for anyone who ever felt under the thumb, unfairly, of authority. Thus, the youth connection! See photo in Appendix, "The Prisoner Ethos."

The Prisoner was 30 years old by the time I met its producer and star, but it still had a magical, almost mystical cachet among its devoted followers. Even today, countless websites, online forums and newsletters attest to its undying popularity. There are guided tours to the site where its exteriors were filmed in Portmeirion, Wales.

Patrick McGoohan had an outstanding acting career both before and since. But he will forever be most remembered for that iconic show. To quote from *The Guardian*'s obituary after Patrick's death in 2009:

> Without *The Prisoner*, we'd never have had cryptic, mindbending TV series like *Twin Peaks* or *Lost*. It's the *Citizen Kane* of British TV – a programme that changed the landscape … Like Orson Welles with *Kane*, McGoohan was given the whole train set to play with on *The Prisoner*, and boy did he play with it.
>
> - *The Guardian,* January 14, 2009.

Patrick the perfectionist

So here I am in 1996, next to Patrick in his hotel suite, on chairs that may or may not be real antiques. He shows me his precious script – at least, what he's written so far. I see the pages number only about 40, which means he's still got a long way to go, as the average feature screenplay numbers between 100–120 pages. The formatting looks passable. He also has a few pages done in longhand on legal-sized paper.

He tells me that he's done the typing at home on his "word-processor" (which I get to see later on; it is about the size of a giant air-conditioner), but hasn't been able to continue here in Montreal. Anyway, he's a hunt-and-peck typist, and typing takes him quite a while. So, he wants me to retype everything into my computer and then work with him on continuing it while he dictates the wording to me, fresh from the horse's mouth, so to speak.

"Sure," I say, "no problem!" Sounds good to me!

He smiles happily. "Wonderful!" he intones loudly. "Why don't you start right over there at the table, set yourself up. Meanwhile I'll look over some t'ings here..." (Patrick would often affect a residual Irish accent. Born in Queens, NY, he grew up in the Republic of Ireland, and England.)

He lights up a skinny cheroot and puffs away; I find an ashtray and fire up one of my own cigarettes. It would be some years before I finally quit the damn things.

I busy myself with my (unfamiliar!) rented Outback computer, finding an outlet, getting comfy in the chair, cushion for my back...

I easily set up the format in Word. I do not have Final Draft, the specialized script formatting software, installed on this laptop. No worries, I've done lots of scripts in Word.

I check with him whether or not he wants the scene headings underlined; he does. And away I go – I'm a speed demon at a keyboard!

After I type about a dozen pages, he asks me from across the room where he's ensconced on the settee, reading, how I'm doing.

"Oh, great!" I say.

"Let's have a look." He comes over and peeks over my shoulder at the screen. I scroll down slowly for him. "Mm-hmm. Mm-hmm. Wait a minute. What's this?!"

"What?" I say, instantly nervous, peering at the typed words.

"Here! Why is the underline like *that?*"

"Uh... wh-what do you mean?"

"Well look. It's squished right up against the letters!!"

I squint. I do see what he means, but – "Oh... but that's the way the program does it," I finish, lamely, not quite getting why it should matter so much. No one else has ever complained.

I am now meeting Patrick the Perfectionist.

"Well it shouldn't look like that! I don't want it squished up like that. Fix it! You're supposed to be the computer expert! You can make anything happen! Isn't that so?"

I feel my stomach falling to the floor. I am terrified, yet trying to act nonchalant at the same time.

"Oh…" I begin, "well sure, I can change it! I'll fix them all…" But my brain is turning somersaults, attempting to imagine how on earth I can circumvent a computer program's set way of doing such a basic thing as underlining. Suddenly I have it!

"I think I'd like to take this home, if you don't mind, and work on it there. I'll take care of the problem, and I'll type all the rest of the pages in. Then when I come back we can continue from there. Um, what do you think?"

The twinkly smile is back, a sight for sore eyes! "All right, good idea! But you'll *fix* it, yeah?"

"Oh yes *of course!*"

You wouldn't believe the pretzel solution I find to the squished-underline problem. Suffice to say it gives the more pleasing appearance he wants, so I'm very relieved to have weathered that little storm. I send a note to his California home later that summer, along with the finished script on a diskette, with an explanation regarding this "pretzel" – just in case someone else tries to continue and/or reproduce my style on the script. It's in the Appendix.

Revelations at the Ritz

When I return to the Ritz to continue our work, I have my precious rented laptop with the up-to-date script now safely tucked into its hard drive. I also have a printout of the pages with me, so Patrick can see that I had indeed "fixed" the underlined scene headings.

As I go to knock on the door, I notice it's partly ajar. I push it open and see not one but two visitors there, both of whom I recognize. The man on the settee talking with Patrick is Bill Brownstein, an entertainment reporter for our English daily, the *Montreal Gazette*. The other visitor is a freelance publicist, Bram Eisenthal, whom I know from having worked on some of the same shows.

Patrick greets me warmly and introduces me to both men, saying, "This is Ellie, she's working with me." I feel pretty important, let me tell you! He lets me know that he's being interviewed and hopes I don't mind waiting a bit. Oh sure – like I *mind* and am going to tell him so! I chat a bit with the publicist, and when it's his turn to talk with Patrick, I go over to the table and set myself up.

After both visitors are gone, I show Patrick the corrected script pages and he is sooo happy. From now on he seems to trust me as someone who knows what she's doing.

Working with Patrick at the Ritz day after day becomes a joy. His script-so-far evokes the same otherworldly, enigmatic ambience as the original series. By now I am clued in to his writing, and even whenever he is stuck for a word and I occasionally dare to suggest one, he accepts it! Now, a non-writer might think, "So what, a word – big deal!" But believe me, the fact that Patrick McGoohan accepts my suggested word is a real coup!

He writes – or I should say dictates – very deliberately. I won't say at a glacial pace; that would be unkind. But he seems to ruminate over every second word; his thoughts are belaboured, sometimes almost tortured. Every sentence or so is an achievement, and then he stops before going on to the next, ordering me: "Read that back to me, Ellie."

I feel self-conscious at first, reading lines back to Patrick, an experienced stage and screen actor, who the hell am I to – but never mind, that's what he wants, so I do it.

He soon learns that *I* could be confidently picky too: We gently argue over the spelling of "woozy." I tell him that it was spelled wrong in his draft; he'd had it as "whoozy." He's doubtful, but I insist. Finally, I tell him I'll "bring in a dictionary, you'll see!" He enjoys my self-assertiveness immensely, chuckling in agreement. When I come back the next day and triumphantly show him "woozy" with no "h," he laughs uproariously.

He seems to get a kick out of me. Go figure.

His laughter helps me relax, and my relaxed state makes me even funnier, which makes him laugh all the more. We enter a cycle of mutual mirth!

Now, it so happens that I've always looked much younger than my age. When it comes out at some point, as we chat a bit between moments of inspiration, that I am 50 years old – he can*not* believe it, sputtering and hooting, "You're not fift-ee-hee-hee!" I just stare at him levelly. "Wanna see my driver's licence?" He guffaws harder.

He has a real mischievous streak. One day I come out of the bathroom in time to hear him on the phone in the living room, saying in his typically loud voice, "Oh, she's *beautiful!*" And he chortles with glee. I come into the room and he immediately looks over at me, saying into the phone, "Yes, oh, ok, she's here, we have to get back to work now," still laughing as he hangs up.

"Patrick!" I yell. "Was that your wife?!"

He nods affirmatively, laughing at his own impishness.

"Why did you tell her I'm beautiful"! He giggles on. I have to explain to this decidedly non-contrite man that no wife wants to hear you're working in your hotel room with a "beautiful" woman, and anyway I'm not beautiful so stop it!

He is infuriating, like a naughty child.

There are a few serious moments too. I ask him how long he's been wearing a beard, and he says many years. I ask him, why not shave it off just for a change? He says, abruptly, "Because I hate my chin!" The subject is closed for discussion. I guess even this much-lauded actor has his insecurities...

Another day, we're working and the phone rings. He answers and I could see by his increasing agitation that it is not someone he cares to speak with. "Listen here," he growls in his gruffest voice, "I don't want you bothering me ever again. Understand? Never again!"

"Oh Ellie," he says, shaking his head. "Don't ever get famous. They don't leave you alone."

****

Over the course of two weeks of working with him, I notice little things around the room that make me wonder: pill bottles, vials of vitamins and potions galore; a bottle of wine or spirits here one day, gone the next.

In any case, after a couple of weeks, we are now almost 70 pages into the script. Patrick tells me that he will soon be leaving for home. And then he goes on to shock me. He wants to continue working on the script with me in California. He wants me to come out to Carmel and stay with him and his wife, Joan, for a while!

I have to remind myself to close my mouth; I think my jaw has fallen to the floor. As he goes on, it becomes clear that he's already thought this through. He says he'd like me to come for 10 days, beginning June 10 – if I am free then.

If I am free? Yep, last time I checked my agenda book, *oh yes indeedy* I am free!

"First class all the way, Ellie," he intones in that stentorian baritone, grinning at me.

California Dreaming Part I – Carmel

June 10, 1996. I have jetted to San Francisco, followed by a hop on a tiny puddle jumper to Monterey. Flying on a 10-seater through the fog isn't a joy – especially after a first-class (free drinks *and* legroom!) experience – but we make it down okay, and I am met by Patrick himself. No one pays us any attention, even though he is so recognizable. My luggage doesn't show up until the next day, but do I really care? I'm here to work with Patrick McGoohan on his script, do I mind a little thing like missing clothes?

Frances, his youngest daughter, drives us to Patrick's home in Carmel, not too far away. She is a beautiful young woman in her 30s. I don't see an immediate resemblance to her dad, and in fact will notice later that she favours her mom.

They drop me off at an upscale motel very near Patrick's house. As he escorts me to my suite, he explains that I would be staying in their own guest house behind their home, except that Frances came in unexpectedly from out of town with her two young children, and they would be occupying it instead. Of course, I am amenable to staying *anywhere* within a hundred miles of Patrick's digs.

Before leaving me in my suite, he hands me an envelope, telling me it contains $3,000 to cover any expenses I have during my stay, and "I expect change," he says, with a fake-menacing tone and evil glint in his eye. He tells me I'm on my own for this evening, but that he will come over tomorrow morning and we'll get started.

I figure $3,000 ought to cover my dinner!

Soon I go out, and walk about a block to Ocean Avenue – it seems to be a main shopping/tourist area, a long street lined with picturesque boutiques and restaurants, wending its way downhill to the Pacific. I'm too tired from travelling to walk that distance, but tuck it away in my "things to do" file in the back of my mind.

For now, I take myself to a nearby pub terrace which has – since it's coolish – outdoor heaters every few feet. This is the first time I've ever seen such things, and am duly impressed. What will they think of next, I marvel. I eat a modest dinner while people-watching, and retire to bed early.

At the agreed-upon time of 11 the next morning, Patrick comes knocking at my motel-room door. I greet him and instantly am grinning – he is wearing a jaunty straw hat and his favourite denim jacket, and looks downright debonair. (Years later I will recognize the jacket when I see him wearing it in a *Columbo* episode!)

We decide (*I* decide, is more like it) that our first order of business will be to go and rent a printer. This means a short drive to Monterey.

Off we go in Patrick's old "boat": it's an ancient Mercedes-Benz, solid as a tank, and huge. I imagine it is as clunky to drive as it looks. We get to Monterey in about 15 minutes (and probably as many gallons of gas). We find a computer store with no trouble; he seems to know exactly where it is... which surprises me, since he's something o f a Luddite.

He comes in with me but after a minute or two, looks uncomfortable, and says he's going to wait outside if I "don't mind." I suspect it's partly because he wants to smoke, which he can't do in here, but also because he is simply overwhelmed and ill at ease among so many high-tech products – which are complete mysteries to him.

After Patrick goes outside, I notice that the clerk seems to have recognized him. I can tell. I know that "Oh my God! It's Number Six!" look.

I tell him what I'm looking for, the compatibility I need, and so on.

Suddenly, he leans over the counter to me and says, conspiratorially, "Do you think Mr. McGoohan would give me an autograph?"

I am tickled! He must think I'm Patrick's assistant – well wait a minute, I sort of *am*, aren't I? I say, "Sure, of course, I'm sure he'll do it!" I figure that even if for some reason he didn't want to, he wouldn't say no, which would make him look mean in front of me.

After a little while Patrick re-enters the store to pay for the printer we're renting. The clerk has gone off to package it. When he comes back with it, grinning, he presents a paper he's holding to Patrick – it's a PR photo of him, the ubiquitous recent PR photo with his trim white beard.

"Oh, look at this," Patrick exclaims, with a smile. "Where'd you get this t'ing?"

"On the Internet," says the clerk proudly, who looks delighted, since the odds of his getting the prized autograph have just gone up exponentially.

"Really, on the Internet? What can't you find on there!" he marvels.

"Here, why don't you sign it, Patrick," I pipe up. "Right there, go ahead," and I hand him a pen. He can't back out now! And indeed, he signs it. I feel like the world's greatest facilitator. Patrick has just made the day – no, year – of one of his biggest fans.

We go back to my motel suite (nothing like the Ritz, but it'll certainly do!) and get set up in the sitting-room area. Luckily, I had brought my laptop to the computer store so we knew everything was compatible and working. (By the way, this was no longer the "Outbound" Mac clone I had rented for our work at the Ritz. I had bought myself a PowerBook 520 before this trip.)

We push ahead with his script for a while and then Patrick leaves, saying he'll pick me up

later and bring me to their place for dinner.
"Very casual," he says.

California Dreaming Part II – Family, food and work

My camera is a useful tool in recording my
visit to Patrick and Joan's house in Carmel. I
take many pictures this evening and in the
ensuing days.

I meet Joan who is a short, pretty little
woman, unassuming and unpretentious, very
sweet. We hit it off immediately. It seems I've
come to know a tiny smidgen of Patrick – the
mischievous, irascible, playful, brilliant man,
who had fallen in love with Joan Drummond,
British stage actress. It was said that he wrote
love letters to her every day, and they married
in 1951. It's a marriage with legs.

I greet their daughter Frances again, and
meet her two young children, Nina and Paddy.
The kids tour the house with Patrick and me as
he shows me every nook and cranny. The place
is beautiful and is decorated everywhere in
bright, airy, pastel tones: pale rose and beige
throughout. Lots of windows, and sunlight
streams in through them on this day.

I am introduced to his pride and joy, his
antiquated word processor, which is about the
size of a small car. Okay, teensy
exaggeration. I have never seen anything like
it! It looks like it even predates the typewriter.

Eventually Joan serves us a delicious

dinner. I am seated at the head of the table, as the guest of honour. We toast each other with white wine, the kids with juice. I announce that henceforth, I am changing my name to "Cinderellie," as this whole trip is like a fairy tale come true. Everyone happily agrees this is most fitting.

Later, just before leaving, as I'm looking at some charming family pictures on a shelf, I peek over to my left and spot a nice little tableau. Patrick is standing in a doorway, swaying ever so slightly, one hand at his chest, as he looks down at Joan. She is talking to him and as she looks up at him, I snap the picture. It seems to exemplify the comfort of a 45-year-old marriage. I also capture a sweet shot of them sitting on a loveseat – a photo I will treasure. (See Photos, Appendix.)

The next day Patrick and I are back at work in my suite. My photos attest to our setup; I'm at the table, he sits on the small settee, script on the seat of the chair in front of him. We sip our coffees, which my suite so kindly provides via a small coffeemaker on a counter.

We take many breaks. Well, *I* call them breaks – we chat, we listen to the radio... but Patrick insists, "This is all work! We're working, you know!" Who am I to argue? But I get it. The brain needs refreshing, replenishing. You can't wear it out.

At one point, we even turn on the TV. I have found in the TV guide a PBS program about the roots of Rock 'n' Roll. We watch the Everly Brothers sing "Kentucky," and are transfixed by their gorgeous harmony. Turns out we are both big fans, and we *love* this song! I tell Patrick I will try to find a recording of it for him.

It's a gorgeous day, and now we want fresh air, so off we go on a walk to the post office. It's a tiny storefront just off Ocean Avenue. I find it odd that no one seems to recognize Patrick, but then I realize this is California, and many famous people are about – heck, the *mayor* is Clint Eastwood (incidentally, Patrick's co-star in *Escape from Alcatraz*) – I suppose it's just taken for granted; no one makes a fuss.

I am on my own for dinner. I find a little Italian place with a terrace tucked behind it, surrounded by flowering greenery and trees – just beautiful. I enjoy my meal, with an open book beside me as a prop. All the other diners seem to be grouped in twosomes, threesomes or more. But I don't care: *I* am an adventurous woman, travelling on my own! Working with Patrick McGoohan!

California Dreaming Part III – Pebble Beach

After a few days of concentrating on the script, Patrick decides we will take a proper break: we will tour the Pebble Beach golf club, and he will treat me to a late lunch. He doesn't play golf there mind you, but he does occasionally go for lunch with one or more of his pals if they're around – Clint Eastwood, Mel Gibson, Peter Falk… but today it'll just be Patrick and me – with me reluctantly driving his monster Mercedes!

"Ellie, you're going to drive. I've had a drink or two, so here you are. I'll tell you where to go," and without further ado he hands me the keys and proceeds to hoist himself into the passenger side.

"But – but I –" I sputter, trying to argue, but it's no use – it's a done deal. I get into the driver's seat and attempt to close the door. It's so heavy, I need to lean over and use all my strength with both hands and yank it shut with a loud *clunk*. I'm hoping it has a manual transmission so I can use the excuse that I absolutely, positively do not know how to drive a standard – but no! Unfortunately for me, it's automatic.

Now in the best of situations, I'm not confident in a car that is strange to me. Someone else's car, or a rental, let's say. But driving this – this *thing,* and in an area, I'm completely unfamiliar with? I'm petrified!

After taking a minute to adjust the mirrors and check where all the buttons and dials are, I start driving, verrry slowly. It feels like I'm driving a recalcitrant train locomotive – with the emphasis on "loco." At the first turn he tells me to make, it seems as if it doesn't even have power steering. Or maybe the fluid level's low. Look, I tell myself, *he* drives it, his *daughter* has driven it, his *wife* probably has driven it, it's *gotta* be safe. I speed up just a tad... so I'm going maybe all of 15 mph now, with gusts to 20.

I stay in the slow lane – when there is one. When there isn't, a line of cars forms behind me, I can see them in the rear-view mirror. I don't care. My hands are gripping the steering wheel so tightly my knuckles are white.

Patrick is oblivious to my plight, looking out the window, humming, telling me occasionally "Turn right next light," or "Stay straight..." We come to a curve. It's a backward "C" and on the inside it's fine, but on the outside there's a cliff, a drop-off – straight down to the ocean! Oh please, God help me! (I'm an atheist but at times like this, well, I tend to hedge my bets.)

Sweating, I slow down to a crawl. I keep the wheel in my death grip turned firmly left. Triumphantly and hugely relieved, I steer us out of the curve (the dead-man's curve as I now think of it). Compared to this, the rest of the drive is no problemo!

Driving into the grounds of the Pebble Beach golf club is akin to going through airport security – minus the passports. This club draws the line at letting in any riff-raff, apparently. *I* am decidedly not riff-raff, driving Patrick McGoohan into the world-famous golf venue in his ancient Mercedes.

Various employees at the clubhouse nod in greeting to Patrick – and to me, by extension.

Good thing I put on my best outfit. It's a pretty turquoise pantsuit with white polka-dots, if you must know. (Look, my mother picked it out and bought it for me before I left Montreal. It's more her taste, not mine, but – well, it's *fresh-looking*.)

We are shown to a table in the dining room – it's the more casual room, not the formal room, Patrick tells me almost apologetically – as if I care! As we wait for our orders, I spring a little surprise on Patrick. I have printed out ersatz cover pages of his script, with the title, "The Prisoner" on each, in the Prisoner typeface,[8] with his name and the date, as well as the Penny Farthing bicycle logo from the show, in the centre. (I'd found it on the Internet of course.)

Well! He is so delighted! "Where'd you find this?!" he exclaims, laughing. I tell him, and then, just as the clerk had asked back in the computer store, I ask if he would mind autographing each page. (I have about six in all: one for me and one for each of my family members.) He signs them, grinning, not minding in the least.

After lunch we meander in the car all over the site, and by now I have to say I am a little less petrified as the road unfurls next to cliffs overlooking the ocean.

Back at my motel, I get out and turn the driving over to Patrick. Just as I was getting

---

[8] It's known unofficially as the "Village" font.

used to being behind the wheel of the behemoth, that's the last I will drive it – but I'm not too sorry.

California Dreaming Part IV – Winding Down

It's the last day of my California stay, and the script is finished. Patrick will take time now to polish his draft before unveiling it to PolyGram. (PolyGram Filmed Entertainment was the company – it folded in 1999 – that was slated to produce a movie from Patrick's *Prisoner* script.)

I spend my last gorgeous (blue-sky-sunny-warm) day on my own, walking down Ocean Avenue, buying little gifts for the McGoohans, heading right down to the beach where I take off my sandals, sit on the sand and watch the waves come rolling in. Ahhhh. I could get used to this.

But the next day it's time for good-byes. Joan and I exchange warm words and hugs. I leave with Patrick and Frances who take me and my luggage to the little airport in Monterey. Patrick reaches down to hug me and I grin up at him and thank him profusely for an amazing stay. I wish him well with the script, which I've given to him on diskette.

****

That was the last time I would ever see him – but not the last time we would speak or write. It was an unforgettable experience having the opportunity to observe this multi-talented man's creative *modus operandi*.

Afterword

A couple of days after I got back home, I sent Patrick a package with this note:

> DATE: June 25, 1996
>
> Hi, Patrick! I hope you're eating, sleeping, and writing – in that order!
> How'd it go with Malibu Mel[9] on Saturday?
>
> I did a silly thing: I walked away (okay, flew away) with the key to my motel room! So here it is; please feel free to return it... or you may want to keep it as a souvenir of our labours!
>
> Also: the search is over! I found an Everly Brothers CD with the song on it. (Actually found two; I'm keeping the other.) Enjoy!

---

[9] Patrick had told me he was going to ask his friend Mel Gibson to play the role of "Number 6" that he himself had played in *The Prisoner* series.

You may be happy to know that Barbara Pruett[10] and I have begun a lively correspondence (by e-mail)! Thanks for "'etting us up"!

Loads of thank-you's once again, love,

Cinderellie xoxoxoxoxoxoetc. - and love to Joan, Frances, Simon, Nina, Paddy

Some weeks later, we spoke on the phone. He was thrilled to receive the CD I sent him of that Everly Brothers song we'd both liked, *Kentucky!*

He was still struggling with the studio over the film and who would star in it, taking his old celebrated role. Mel Gibson passed. Patrick told me that it would be a 65-million-dollar film, a lot of dough at the time. For comparison, the 1995 James Bond film *Goldeneye* had a budget of $58 million. That $65-million budget might have been a bit of a stumbling block, especially for PolyGram, which was beginning to go through some difficulties.

Maybe part of the problem was Patrick's script, which was quite cerebral, much like his original series – light-years away from the typical Hollywood shoot-'em-up.

As he angrily spat out the words to me on the phone, "They want explosions, Ellie! Car

---

[10] A big fan of his who had become a friend.

chases!!" And I could hear him snort in disgust, over the phone line, 3,000 miles away.

Months later I faxed him a cheery Christmas note:

> Dear Patrick,
>
> All my best wishes to you and your gorgeous family: Joan, Frances, Simon, Nina, Paddy, and to the others. I didn't get to meet them all last summer, but what the heck, they know who they are!
>
> I hope you're feeling well... I've been thinking a lot about you lately. As I do script revisions on this new series I'm working on, characterized as "erotic horror" – don't ask! – I occasionally peek at your script here for a breath of fresh air, so to speak.
>
> Finished watching all 17 eps of *The P.*, shown on Bravo recently. I think my favourite is "Hammer into Anvil," for its great portrayal of progressive paranoia... Oh yeah, you were pretty good too. <grin>
>
> Any news re the film? (I guess not, or you would have told me...)

Well, I hope you have a lovely, warm
family holiday.

Love, xoxoxo Ellie

****

I received a nice-but-generic Season's
Greetings card back from him, addressed to
"Cinderellie," signed, "Patrick."

Our last contact was the fax I sent him
two years later:

MESSAGE: DATE: JAN16/98

DEAR PATRICK COMMA MISS
YOUR LAUGH STOP SAW
SUNDAY TIMES ARTICLE STOP
DON'T GIVE IN LONG DASH NOT
EVEN ONE WOOZY LITTLE
EXPLOSION EXCLAMATION
POINT LOVE XOXOX ELLIE

That "DON'T GIVE IN" admonishment
refers to the article I'd seen, in which Patrick
was lamenting the intransigence of the studio –
they were still insisting that much more
firepower and bloodshed should be inserted into
his script.

In 1998, PolyGram Filmed Entertainment
was sold to Universal Pictures and folded in
1999. Karma, I'd say.

Rumours abounded over the years since

then, regarding the fate of Patrick's script, whether there even *was* a script, or who the various directors/cast members/writers were. Finally, a remake of the TV series came out in 2009 as a miniseries, with Ian McKellen and Jim Caviezel. I did not see it.

For me and countless others, there will only ever be one "Prisoner"... and unfortunately, the man who embodied the show died January 13, 2009 following a long illness. Sad to say, his script – his labour of love – died with him.

PART SIX - THE HUNGER

Our driver has no car!

It was, as usual, a tough day at the production offices of *The Hunger,* Season One, 1997. Two episodes were in post, one was shooting in the studio downstairs, several were undergoing various stages of pre-prod – and I had a front-row seat to the action in my pivotal role as script coordinator. I was also an assistant to one of the show's consultants, who was now shoving some VHS tapes and pages in my hands, urging me to get them over to head office a few blocks away. It was there that the office of Téléscene's bigwigs were located – the top exec producers of the show, the head of creative affairs, and the like.

Picture the frenzy that this anthology show was steeped in: time constraints, of course – one episode shot every week, filmed as a mini-movie – a new director and story every week. New sets to be constructed. Different cast and many of the crew, too. Every. Single. Week. In the first season alone (22 half-hour episodes), we burned through two heads of production and several production managers, as well as numerous production coordinators and secretaries. Oh, the pressure! You had to grin and bear it – or go nuts and quit. I grinned and bore it… most of the time.

And now here was "Marvin," my immediate boss, one of the creative consultants, cramming tapes and pages in my hand, telling me to get them to head office pronto! I said I'd do it, stuffed them into a manila envelope and rushed them over to Matt, our office driver.

Uh-oh! Not good. I dashed back down the corridor to Marvin with the news. He wasn't gonna like this.

"What?!! What are you saying?!!" he shouted, as expected.

I repeated it, trying to stifle my laughter: "Our driver," I said, "has no car."

Thankfully he also saw the humour in it.

Matt finally found someone's car to borrow (someone else had taken *his!), and* the mini-crisis was over, but meanwhile we had a good chuckle out of it, and I got an excellent title for a book chapter.

****

The Hunger, a TV series produced by Téléscene along with Tony and Ridley Scott's company, Scott Free, for Showtime, was predicated on the interplay of two genres: horror (with supernatural elements), and erotica. Erotic horror, if you will. I see nothing erotic about cannibalism or garden-variety murder, but that's just me!

Here's a blurb I wrote in the first season describing the show:

Bizarre. Erotic. Horror. This is *The Hunger*, a drama anthology of half-hour episodes, a co-venture of Scott Free Productions – Tony and Ridley Scott's U.K. production company, Showtime Networks Inc. in the U.S., and Téléscene Communications of Montreal.

The first two episodes were shot in London, England last fall, and the rest are being filmed in Montreal through to mid-May. Each show is based on a published short story by a respected author such as Harlan Ellison, Edgar Allan Poe or Brian Lumley.

Rising high-profile directors such as Patricia Rozema *(I've Heard the Mermaids Singing, When Night is Falling)*, Russell Mulcahy *(Highlander III, The Shadow)*, Christian Duguay *(Million-Dollar Babies, Screamers)* and George Mihalka *(La Florida, L'homme idéal)* have signed on to helm at least one episode each. Tony Scott himself is directing the wraparound segments featuring Terence Stamp and David Bowie.

The Hunger is an edgy, sophisticated series that explores the conflicts between fear and desire, and the ecstatic heights and depths of human obsession. Each story will be shot over five days with a distinct visual style usually unique to features. The budget for each episode is

$708,000 U.S.

Executive producers include, besides Ridley and Tony Scott: creator Jeff Fazio – the writer who brought the original concept to their attention – and Téléscene's Robin Spry, Paul Painter and Bruce Moccia.

Showtime has ordered 22 episodes for the first season that starts airing in June 1997.

The beginning

I was called to work on the show in the winter of 1996-97. It followed neatly on the heels of my *Space Cases* second season. On the appointed day, two other women and I showed up to meet with Jeff Fazio, creator and exec producer. A rather unassuming man, Jeff seemed to be in a panic. We soon learned this was his natural state. (To be fair, this L.A. denizen had a lot on his plate – finding quality writers, directors and cast for twenty-two episodes in Season One, and another 22 in Season 2 – all the while chafing at tight budget restrictions.) I distinctly recall that the four of us met standing in the doorway of his office.

He said he was in dire need of a personal assistant, a creative assistant, and a script coordinator. Which of us wanted to do which job? He apparently expected us to decide this among ourselves, while we were all standing there. Seriously?

Well, of course I piped up and said I was an experienced script coordinator, and that was *definitely* what I wanted to do. The other two split the remaining job offers between them – although in another month, only one of them would be left, the other gone the way of *Hunger* casualties.

Later, after some discussion with Jeff about the software I would use, and the method or flow of work involving my tasks, I managed to manoeuvre things my way. That is, I would use my own Mac Powerbook along with the wonderfully flexible Final Draft program, my favourite at that point. The goal? By the time the writers – several in-house writers were alternately used – had reached their production-draft stage, they would pass their scripts to me on diskettes. I would then format them properly in Final Draft, since most of the writers were still using Word or (shudder) Wordperfect! This software helped me do all formatting functions automatically, such as the all-important page-locking. (I don't mean to shill for Final Draft in particular; later I discovered another program that did the job just as well – it was called Screenwriter.)

I also proofread the scripts and fixed typos. If I saw any bigger gaffes, I would give notes on them to the writer. For instance, I might have told them that No, you can't say Arnie pours the wine in Scene 6, since you killed him off in Scene 4. Okay, that's a tad simplified, but you get the idea. Basically, I was saving the writers from embarrassing themselves.

After the pages were locked, the script was now known as a Production Draft, also called a Table Draft, since it is the version used when cast members first read it around a table at a "table read." (A table read is also sometimes called a read-through, or read-thru, for lazy spellers.) At that point, I became the sole keeper of the up-to-date script, and changes would be fed directly to me all the way through the end of the production. As I alluded to in earlier chapters, we could be on DOUBLEGOLDENROD coloured pages by the end of the shoot!

A note about the writers: if you look at the Cast and Crew page at *The Hunger*'s entry in the IMDb, you'll see a whole whack o' them. That's misleading. The regular in-house writers were only the first four in the list. All the rest were the writers of the original short stories that the episodes are based on; almost none of them went on to write the screenplays.

Aside from processing script revisions and keeping track of all versions, I drew up and disseminated (in Season One, at least) agendas and minutes for weekly story team meetings. Here's an early set of minutes; it gives you a good overview of the complex behind-the-scenes juggling that went on.

STORY TEAM MEETING
MINUTES

<u>Jan. 24/97</u>
1. <u>Shih-Tan</u>

- Jeff, Marvin, Jerry to review the Blue.
Jeff then will confer with Russell at 4:30
today re Yellow changes.
- Ellie will publish Yellow tonight.
- Read-thru: Sunday, Jan. 26, here, at 3:00.

2. The Other Woman
- Ellie to publish Marvin's 3rd draft.
- Showtime notes due; Robin's notes due;
George's notes due. Jeff & Marvin to
discuss after they're read.
2.1 Beautiful Vampire
- Jerry will have 2nd draft ready Mon. Jan.
27.
2.2 Bridal Suite
- Marvin to read it; to be discussed
Monday.

3. Start David Shore
- conference call arranged: today, 6:00
p.m. our time, for David, Jeff & Marvin, re
Matter of Style.

4. Start Bruce Smith on Monday.
- re Sloan Men. Jeff to call, re meeting
with him to give him direction. Get him
here Monday. Confirm that he has a copy
of Sloan Men.

5. More stories. (Graham's now)
- After J, M & J pick new potential stories,
copies should go to Mark Nelson &
Showtime.
-Showtime should get a 1/2 page summary
(pitch re our take) attached to each
potential story. (Marvin to do?)

- Possibles:
Heart to Heart (Jeff to read)
Lighthouse (Marvin to read it. Jerry to do
pitch for Showtime.)
Triangle and Steel (Marvin to read.)
Pagan Rabbi (needs pitch. Jerry? Marvin?)
Tim Hunter sending us a story.
Marvin's bringing in a story.
Anita's reader, Dawn, to check several
anthology series e.g. Barbara Gowdy;
Gemma Files stories
Lady Luck is GONE.
- Debra to put copies of potential stories
into binders for: Jeff, Marvin, & Jerry.

6. Hidebound
- Showtime passed - BUT Jeff wants to
make a case for it (esp'y to Bruce Moccia.)
6.1 Anais
- Showtime wants a one-pager. (Marvin to
read story, and do it.)

7. Procedures
- Story team to meet every Friday at 11:30.
- Ellie to maintain & publish schedules.
(timeline; story dev't & rights status) to
team plus Robin & Anita (& Diane &
Christian G. too?)
- Debra to help re miscellaneous tasks.
- all team should get copies of
EVERYthing we have! (e.g. all stories
being considered, memos, schedules,
outlines, notes, script versions etc.)

8. New writers

Dubois
- Réné Paul Dubois (Qc) (wrote Being at Home With Claude): coming here Jan. 27? He submitted a script which Marvin will read. We'll try to get him approved by Showtime.

John Hamilton
- Quebec writer (wrote Myth of the Male Orgasm) - Jeff to talk to him.

9. Directors
- Jeff looking after. Under consideration: Duguay, Canuel, Beaudin, Simoneau, Wasyk...etc.
- Tom Dey (Vampire) arriving here Tuesday (Jan. 28)?

10. Publication
A) Small publication: Jeff, Marvin & Jerry; Robin & Anita.
B)Showtime.
C)All.

Submitted by Ellie Presner
cc
Robin
Jeff
Marvin
Jerry
Ellie
Debra
Sylvie Normandin
Scott Free

Telescene
Showtime

All this doesn't even take into account the episodes that had advanced to that other crazy world known as post-production. That was yet to come! It's no wonder this undertaking was so exhausting.

In addition to script revisions, version tracking, dissemination, agendas and story-meeting minutes, I also dealt with memos detailing new writers and clearances, loglines, and all sorts of other internal notes and faxes, in that age before emails were commonplace. I also was on the lookout for short stories that could be adapted for our series. I covered a few but they weren't really suitable. "Covering" a story in this context means giving a synopsis of the tale and pointing out why it would make a good episode – or why it wouldn't.

On top of all that, I was conscripted as an assistant to the new exec creative consultant on the show. Most of it involved negligible tasks like making his dinner reservations (only at the best restos in town, mind you) ... and helping him— every Friday – clean off his paper-strewn desk. How thrilling it was to see the wooden top of his tidied desk again! I was *so* delighted on his behalf.

It's okay Marvin, I really enjoyed it, and you... except for the time you lost your temper when your car got stuck in the snowy driveway and your bellowing caused heads to peek (in fear and trembling) out of offices all up and down the corridor, looking for the rage source. Whatever. Overall, you meant well. The fact that you needed anger-management lessons, hey, we all have our quirks.

Surviving with humour

To break up the tension of the daily grind, I founded what I called the H. H. A. – The Hunger Humour Administration. The main role of this august body (which consisted of, er, me!) was to generate silly memos. What can I say? They made me laugh while writing them. Here's one I wrote and distributed:

NEW CRAFT PARAMETERS

1. A ceiling of 93 bagels per day.

2. Poppy seed bagels and sesame seed bagels must be equal in number. Cutting them in half is encouraged.

2.1 If special flavours are desired, e.g. cinnamon-raisin-hazelnut, clearance must be obtained prior to purchase.

3. No more than 1.7 varieties of danish.

3.1 Sharing danish is recommended.

4. Paper-towel usage must be curtailed. Try tearing the sheets in half. Better yet, use the ratty old towel [preserved in its original state since Urban Angel[11] hanging near the sink.

5. No more than 572 pots of coffee a day. It is appreciated that restraint in this area will be extremely difficult; however, everyone's cooperation is necessary in order to make our kitchen cost-effective.

6. Re: drinks: glass bottles are to be saved in order to be melted down to create windows for the ADs' office (and Chris Dalton's office, if there is enough glass left over).

6.1 From now on, only one brand of soft drink will be permitted: "Jolt." Remember their motto: "Twice the sugar, four times the caffeine!"

Thank you for your collaboration.

by order of the H.H.A.*

*Hunger Humour Administration.

****

---

[11] A show also produced by Téléscene back in 1991.

Did anyone laugh when they read this? I didn't know; I was just having a great time! Here's another. (I've changed the names in this one – just because.)

EASTER BUNNY DUTIES

It has come to the attention of the H.H.A. that Friday, March 28 is Easter (Good Friday). The following should be noted:

1. Jim O'Day would make a fine Easter Bunny. The costume department should be careful, however, to keep the tail down to 8" in diameter. Any excess tailage will be severely reprimanded. And besides, Jim wouldn't be able to sit down if it were any larger.

2. In the event that Jim O'Day is unavailable for Easter Bunny duty, Arnold Kleindigger would make a perfect runner-up. (But I'm not gonna tell him. Are you??)

3. In the unlikely event that neither Jim nor Arnold is available for Bunny duty, whom would you recommend? Please write legibly in the spaces below.

Thank you for your collaboration.

****

Just one more. And then I'll stop, I promise.
This was from Season 2; I only shared it with
those closest to me. You'll see why!

TOP TEN RULES FOR
THE HUNGER EPISODES:

10. In every episode, the leading man
must scream.
9. It's the leading woman's fault.
8. His screams are due either to:
   a/ death by vacuum cleaner

   b/ death by puppet

   c/ death by flower seeds

   d/ death by green-screen fall

7. It's the leading woman's fault.

6. Every leading woman reaches sexual
fulfillment in .9 seconds.

5. It's the leading man's great skills that
make this possible.

4. Condom? What condom??

3. The more famous they are, the less
naked they get.

2. Only sexy lesbians have sex.

And the number one rule for a
Hunger episode:

1. Women are evil. Men are just
stupid.

Table Reads – making myself useful

Table reads were fun. Well, at least for me. I got to see the actors dramatically read the script as they sat around a conference table. Any changes in wording that were suggested and accepted, I would scribble onto my hard copy of the script, later to type them in and distribute to cast and crew on coloured A & B pages. I vividly remember a few of these sessions.

We were having a read-thru for "But At My Back I Always Hear," an episode based on a short story by David Morell. As described on the IMDb, it was about "a university professor [who] rejects an advance made by one of his students and discovers that her twisted obsession with him does not end with her death."

The professor was played by Michael Gross, famous for his role as Michael J. Fox's dad in the beloved long-running TV series, *Family Ties*. Here he was to do a fine job in a dramatic role that called for a large dollop of paranoia.

At this read-thru the room was packed. Cast and key production people were all there; for once there was no room for me to sit at the table, so I made myself comfy on the floor. As it happens I was right behind the director, Patricia Rozema, and a couple of feet from Michael Gross.

The read was going along merrily when they came to a point in the script where Michael is talking with his "wife," trying to downplay the reason for his unhinged student phoning him all the time. (There's a bit of guilt involved on his part, since he did "give in" on one occasion to the girl's charms. Just the once, mind you! Hunger trysts were most often instigated by the female. Evil Jezebels every one!)

Michael reads, "She – she thinks she's in *love* with me or something."

He doesn't look happy... and tries again. "She's in *love* with me. Hmm... um..."

He's clearly not thrilled with this line, and looks like he smells something a bit off. "Um... She's... She..."

I pipe up from the floor, "She has a CRUSH on me!"

Ah ha!! All heads swivel around and down to me, the source of this brilliance, but best of all is Michael who juts out his arm and points at me, exclaiming, "Yes! That's it! She has a *crush* on me!"

Patricia turned around and looked down, scowling, at me on the floor behind her. What's the mere script coordinator doing, contributing a line? I didn't care. Oh, did I mention she had written this episode? Some writers were *very* protective of their turf.

When Michael said "my" line as I later watched the episode on tape, I admit it gave me a little thrill.

At another table read, along came Sally Kirkland, a real character if there ever was one.

An escaped walking time warp from the fifties, this erstwhile blonde bombshell swept into our offices with her cute little dog in tow. Guess who volunteered to be dogsitter – dog wrangler, if you will, during the read? Look, I love dogs, okay?

I went and got him a big bowl of water, and cuddled him while the actors did their thing. Sally did a great job in "Bridal Suite," playing a murderous *Arsenic-and-Old-Lace* type, the elderly owner of a B&B who just *loved* her honeymooning guests. (Hopefully she kept her dogs around longer than the people!)

Another time I met Margot Kidder, who came to portray one of the strange characters in the "Sloan" family. She was very friendly to me, totally down to earth, unlike many other actors I'd met over the years, some of whom you just feel like shaking and telling them to get over themselves. We were the only two punctual people in the room that day, it seemed. So, I stuck out my hand and introduced myself. She shook it and warmly said, "Call me Maggie."

"Maggie" still had the young-girl demeanour of her famous Lois Lane character in the first four Superman films. We made small talk until the rest of cast and crew filed into the room.

Many other memorable actors came to star in *Hunger* episodes. The casting department made some good decisions: Giancarlo Esposito (pre-"Gus" from *Breaking Bad*), Chad Lowe, Karen Black, Balthazar Getty, Jason Scott Lee,

Esai Morales, Jennifer Beals, Anthony Michael Hall, Lena Headey, Giovanni Ribisi, even Daniel Craig – and many others. Not necessarily many "A" actors at the time, but certainly many talented ones, and some even destined for life in the "A" category later on.

The two biggest stars, Terence Stamp and David Bowie, had roles in the "Wraparounds": Stamp in the first season, Bowie in the second. "Wraparound" refers to the introduction and epilogue of every episode. They were shot separately from the episodes they "wrapped around" and were edited in later, before and after each. Bowie also starred in one of the episodes, "Sanctuary." (And of course, he had had a starring role in the original 1983 movie, *The Hunger,* which Tony Scott directed.) Aside from seeing these actors fleetingly in the corridor (Stamp) or on the set (Bowie), I did not get to rub shoulders with them. The ones that got away. Sigh.

Writers – a sensitive bunch

Now I'll recount a few things I discovered about screenwriters, but I'll keep it general as I don't want to denigrate the talents or characters of any of these fine gentlemen. So, I will just say this: some writers are very insecure. During the first season when I sat in on story meetings, there was one writer who became very annoyed if I ever opened my mouth to contribute a word or, heaven forbid, an actual *idea.* He would absolutely glare at me, if I ever dared to speak up. Metaphorical poison darts shot from his eyes towards me.

Since I didn't want any lingering antagonism between us, I once went to him after a meeting and said, "Um, 'Larry,' it seems to bother you whenever I contribute to the discussion."

"Yeah, it puts me off. Don't do it, it puts me off."

Well, far be it from me to "put off" poor Larry. So, I shut up from then on, whenever it was one of his scripts being discussed. I also noticed that, alone among the regular writers, Larry would obsessively read over his drafts about ten times before leaving them with me to format – and *after* I formatted them, to make sure I hadn't changed anything I wasn't supposed to, perhaps!

I recall on another show, a feature, the writer dictated changes to me word by painful word, as he stood behind me while I typed. At one point, he was stumped. He stood there swaying, mired in the depths of indecision. My brain was roiling with a dozen or more possibilities to suggest. Finally, I could stand it no longer, and one of the synonyms I'd thought of fairly burst forth from my lips.

"I'M the writer!" he exclaimed. Whoaaa! Okay! Once again, a writer hobbles himself out of spite, for fear of being "shown up" by a lesser mortal. In my opinion, the script is the thing, no? If I want to help make it better, why not?

It's *your* name going on there, not mine, so *you'll* get the credit for it, *you'll* look good! Don't you want to look good? Don't you want the *script* to be good? But of course I could say none of these things.

Back to *The Hunger* writers: many was the time I thought I was working with fearful and vengeful little children instead of talented adults who should've been supremely confident, having landed this great gig... no? Well no, instead, I was party to things like running each other down behind each other's backs: "He's an old-time hack." "He's a little boy." "He's a weasel, he can't write." "Do you think so-and-so's mad at me?" "I have nobody to hate now. Who can I hate?" "I abhor exclamation points!"

The job jar

When I wasn't working on actual script revisions, attending meetings or churning out agendas, minutes, faxes and memos (humorous or otherwise), I had a whole panoply of other duties, including:

- Script schedules – These were charts showing the episode title, director, writer, date each revision was due, etc. They were invaluable for everyone, from creative folks to those on the business end.
- Inventories – These were lists of the

demo tapes in Jeff's office, i.e.
tapes he used to help assess which
actors and directors he wanted to
tap for our show; also lists of movie
tapes – again, to help him with
hiring decisions.

- Distribution – Who gets what,
  when and, no less important, *how*.
  In their cubby? By fax? Email?
  (We were just at the cusp of the
  email era.) Courier? Our driver? (If
  he had a car!)
- Liaising with various key
  personnel in other departments
  e.g. legal (clearances, contracts);
  Showtime; Scott Free.

****

The next season of *The Hunger* brought
new challenges and changes.

Second season shenanigans, featuring Tony Scott

The biggest change for me was that in
Season 2, as I was rehired by our excellent line
producer Christian Gagné, I told him I did not
want to be Marvin's assistant this time.
(Between you and me, if I had to endure his
Friday-afternoon desk clean-ups or make his
ritzy dinner reservations one more time, I was

gonna lose it.)

This was my job description as I drew it up in 1998 at the start of Season II:

- Keeping track of status of all scripts
- Overseeing receipt of new drafts
- Formatting and proofreading new drafts on computer
- Taking notes of script changes during read-thrus as needed
- Entering all script revisions on computer
- Monitoring distribution of script versions
- Maintaining files of hard copies of all script versions
- Creation and distribution of script/production schedules
- Creation and distribution of agendas and minutes for story-team meetings as necessary
- Misc. memos as necessary
- Liaison with other departments as necessary
- Misc. tasks, e.g. faxing, filing etc. if/when time permits

When I greeted Marvin as he arrived on his first day of the new season, rarin' to go, I informed him that I would no longer be his assistant. He turned a not-unattractive shade of purple; violet, really. "What?!" was all he could choke out. He rushed from his office down the hall to talk to Christian. I saw them through Christian's glass office door – a heated exchange seemed to be going on.

I avoided eye contact with Marvin for a while after that, and then a few days later, who do I see gracing *Hunger* offices? A new employee, an affable young fellow named Michael – Marvin's brand-spanking-new assistant. I spoke to him briefly – he was *very* young and absolutely thrilled to have landed this position, which, as was the case with most of us, was obtained via someone who knew someone.

Well that's good, I thought. Marvin got what he wanted. However, there was one bit of fallout from this, which was very disconcerting to me. Guess who was no longer expected to attend the always-interesting story meetings, and guess who went instead? No points. Too easy!

But my disappointment was mitigated by other perks. Most days I was finished work by 6:00. This was considered very early by production-office standards, since many people slaved away until much later at night (not counting those who worked on set, where 14-16+ hour days were not uncommon). More than once I was teased as I was leaving, with comments like, "Ohh, Ellie, bankers' hours, eh?!" It didn't bother me; I thought it was funny, and besides, my work was done for the day, and by now I was pretty much indispensable to the production. Well, as indispensable as anyone *can* be in this crazy business, I suppose. (Which is to say, not very. Ultimately, anyone can be replaced.)

I enjoyed my work environment this time more than that of the previous season. I now shared an office with Jeff's assistant, Sylvie, along with the post- production coordinator, Sia. The three of us got along famously as we shared a similar (silly!) sense of humour as well as musical tastes. On slower afternoons, we'd listen to some great songs on our little portable radio, in those pre-iPod days. Sylvie taught me all the lyrics to the Proclaimers' "500 Miles." For some reason, we loved that song and played it over and over!

My officemates also kept me apprised of juicy gossip, such as the fact that one of the production accountants had a fling with one of the actors (Anthony Michael Hall, if you *must* know.). Rumour had it that she was so smitten that she later flew down to L.A. to visit him, some time after he'd returned there from doing his episode. Rumour also had it that he was, to put it mildly, rather surprised to see her – and not in a good way. Oh dear.

****

One of my most memorable experiences came one night towards the end of Season 2. It was during the last month or so, and director Tony Scott was in town to shoot the episode he was going to direct – "Sanctuary," which starred David Bowie – as well as the "Wraparounds." It was during his pre-production phase, and one night Jeff's assistant Sylvie and I were both working late. (Well, late for me!)

Around 9 or 10 p.m., Jeff came into our office and invited Sylvie and me out for a late dinner with Tony and himself... and the storyboard artist, Marie.

Sylvie begged off for some reason, I can't recall why. But as for me? *Hell* yes, count me in!

By the time we got downtown to a super-trendy restaurant, it was close to 11 p.m. A late dinner indeed! Well, this being rockin' Montreal, the uber-edgy place was jam-packed, but somehow we got a table. Did Jeff give a very greasy tip to the maitre d'? Could be.

In any case, Jeff and Marie and Tony and myself were seated at a table for four – and promptly had to converse in sign language, or by yelling, since the noise level was not to be believed! I have never been in a restaurant as noisy before or since! A bar or club, yes, but not a resto. Mind you, it *had* a bar there which was extremely popular; I could see people crammed in front of it about five deep. Tony was sitting right next to me and we were trying to have a conversation but it was so difficult. I had to lean over with my ear right next to his mouth.

Service as you might expect in such a packed place was interminably slow. Finally, my pasta dish came. It took so long that I wasn't really hungry by then. You know that stage where you're beyond hunger pangs? This was it. (How ironic, *The Hunger* people out to eat – but they're not hungry!)

You also may imagine that the wine was going straight to my head. I started thinking and feeling things towards Tony. My loopy brain was a-buzz with thoughts like, "Here we are, the four of us – arrayed as two couples. Jeff & Marie. Tony & Ellie. Hmm. Wifey is far away, way back in L.A. *Do* they all fool around, I asked myself?"

The next thing my woozy brain registered, we were out on the sidewalk in front of the restaurant. My plan was to hail a cab and go home where I could fall into bed. Jeff had other ideas.

"Come Ellie, we're just going to a club down there," as Jeff gestured a bit north. "It's a cigar lounge. Come with us!" He and Marie and Tony were starting to walk towards the place, but they turned back towards me – it was almost like he was *begging* me to come with them. I kept saying no, no, but he kept cajoling!

By now it was 1:00 a.m. and I was dying of fatigue. And part of me was thinking, what is the point of doing that? It will only push me closer to Tony. And I do not want him to get the wrong idea. I like him, but... (I was super-averse to sleeping with married men.) Finally, Jeff very reluctantly gave up. We said goodbye and went our separate ways.

The last time I saw Tony was later on at the Hunger offices, as he meandered down the hall in his trademark cap and baggy tights. What a character, I thought to myself.[12]

Spoilers

Oh, I don't mean "spoilers" in the traditional sense, where I tell you details of the episodes that will spoil the surprises. No, I'm referring to things that happened that "spoiled" any spirit of cooperation on the show, that might have been in play in Season 2.

Sad to say, during this second go-around the rift between production and creative people began to widen and never stopped. The creative camp, led by Jeff Fazio who had initiated the series, along with Tony Scott at Scott Free, insisted on being firmly in charge of all creative work – the cinematography, editing, cast, directors, score, costumes, locations – i.e., all the elements that went into the production. In the other corner of the ring (as it were) sat the production people concerned with the budget – the *runaway* budget! These included the

---

[12] Sadly, notwithstanding Tony Scott's tremendous success in the film world (www.imdb.com/name/nm0001716/), he committed suicide in 2012. He was 68.

producers at Téléscene, who were responsible for the entire local crew and the costs – costs that were but annoying mosquito bites to Jeff and Tony.

Line producer Christian, along with consultant Marvin, on the other hand, were *very* concerned with costs that were threatening to spiral out of control completely. Gradually an us-vs.-them mentality took root and started to spread: production vs. creative; art vs. money.

On most shows, especially in the U.S., there is clearly someone in charge of all these factors; that person is called a showrunner.[13] But on *The Hunger,* the lines were blurred. There were times when Jeff and Marvin each seemed to fancy himself as the showrunner. It was pretty messy, to tell you the truth.

Everyone's nerves, including mine, were frayed by the last few weeks of production. One day I went and knocked perfunctorily on Marvin's door – which was open, mind you. I just knocked to be polite. He was typing on his laptop. His shoulders sagged as he stopped, looked up and saw me. Immediately he got that expression on his face that said, "Oh cripes, what the hell does she want now?!" This came on the heels of other instances wherein I was starting to feel distinctly unappreciated.

Also, let it be known that I seldom interrupted him. But now I had an important question on a script.

I was instantly seized by frustration – and a

---

[13] https://en.wikipedia.org/wiki/Showrunner

feeling like, "What am I, chopped liver?!" I whirled around and hurled myself into my office, closed the door (a tad not-so-gently) and sat down in a huff at my desk. Fatigue and irritation – not a great combo. I could feel the tears leaking out as I rubbed my eyes like a little kid. I really felt like screaming but drew the line there.

Next thing I knew there was a quiet knock on the door. Ha, guess who?! Marvin entered, hesitating, "Can I… come in…?" I could see an apology was coming.

Yep! "Look, I'm sorry, it's just – you know – we're winding down… it's not easy…"

I glared at him. "Why do you have to treat me like *shit?!*" I spat.

Wow. As I remember this, I'm astounded at how angry I was, and – I'm thinking maybe – just maybe – I overreacted. Nerves on edge I suppose, like everyone else, by now.

He apologized, and then we actually had a decent conversation… until we didn't. He was telling me of the difficulties arising from the cross-purposes of production *needs* vs. creative *wants*. I said something I thought showed great understanding and empathy, something to the effect of, "It must be tough being number two –"

He exploded, "I'M NOT NUMBER TWO!!"

Oh, I said (to myself, wisely), could've fooled me! Apparently, he did not consider himself to be lower on the credits totem pole than Jeff. Funny, I thought, one has only to look at the crew list[14] to see that he's not the first name on there.

The last weeks of the show saw relations between almost everyone deteriorating. (Notable exception – my officemates and I were still close.)

One day a loud argument between Christian and Jeff began to get out of hand. Christian was just leaving Jeff's office and apparently (I couldn't make out exactly what was being said) words had escalated to the point of no return. I had a front-row seat, so to speak, to what followed. They both began to scuffle in the hallway, as Sylvie and I watched – mesmerized – from our doorway. They were both itching to take a swing at each other, but were holding each other at arm's length to keep from being on the receiving end.

By now, Marvin was out of his office, watching, helpless. Others, too. Brave little Sylvie, weighing maybe 100 pounds soaking wet, stepped forward, yelling, "Jeff! Stop it! Stop it both of you!!" She actually tried to physically separate them. I was terrified, watching this, worried for her in the middle, and for the men, so furious – I pressed my fists to my mouth in horror. Finally, they broke apart when Christian twisted to his right and *punched a hole in the wall!*

---

[14] Or now on the Internet Movie Database: www.imdb.com/name/nm0001716/

Yikes! The hole in the plaster remained there for a couple of days, a testament to the frustration and craziness of this whole production. We'd just look at it in dismay and shake our heads.

Then one day someone from the carpentry gang was dispatched to fill the hole and paint it over. Too bad people's feelings couldn't be smoothed over as easily.

****

That fight led right into another one (less violent – at least physically)! This time I was more involved. I call it the Script Standoff.

As I've mentioned, the last script to be filmed was Tony's episode. It was written by Bruce M. Smith and was to be directed by Tony. By now, budgetary concerns had reached epic proportions. Things had devolved into two camps: Christian and Marvin, favouring budget restraint, vs. Jeff and Tony – money be damned – we're making art!

The script for "Sanctuary" was given to me on diskette by its creator, Bruce M. Smith. Immediately, Jeff came in to warn me that *no* way was I to show this script to Marvin. This would be very unusual; Marvin would always read over first drafts to see if he thought they could use some editing. But by this time, Marvin was seen by Jeff as sort of a traitor to the cause of art; he was – a sin! – aligned more with Christian and the dictates of the wallet.

But I told Jeff, sure, okay. He was the creator and executive producer on the show, after all. I bit my lip with anxiety. I knew this wasn't gonna be pleasant.

Sure enough, just a few minutes later, Marvin walked into my office. He must've seen Bruce come in and then leave. "You got the script," he said, more like a statement than a question.

"Er, yes."

"Okay, let's see it."

"I – I can't... show you."

"What do you mean!"

"I... was told not to."

"WHAT?!? I *have* to see it!!!"

I shrank, shaking. (I hated confrontation!)

"Lemme see it!!"

"I'm not allowed to give it to you!!"

"Who toldyou?!"

(No big secret) "Jeff," I said, in my tiniest voice.

Of course, Marvin exclaimed something like "Ugh!" and whipped out of my office, to confront him, wherever, whatever, oh, I was so sick of the infighting now!

The rift had widened to a chasm. Jeff had his way; he "banned" Marvin from all further contact with the script, with Tony, with anything to do with this last episode.

Marvin was thus left with not much to do but seethe. As I recall, he departed before the wrap party, probably (justifiably) disgusted with his treatment at the end of the show's run.

(Personally, I always tended to think along the lines of Rodney King: "Can we all get along?")

One nice thing

I feel I owe it to Marvin to mention one nice thing he did for me. It happened about a year after I was diagnosed with multiple sclerosis, in 1998. (I know that's coming out of left field, but it's been, luckily, extremely mild and never hampered my activities. Often, I forget I have it! However, back then I started using a cane for a while just in case.) When Marvin saw me with the cane, he ventured that he thought it was too big for me, that is, too high for my 5-foot-tall frame.

"Let me get it shortened for you," he offered.

When I hesitantly agreed (Why is he being so nice to me, I wondered), he took it and disappeared for about half an hour. He came back, smiling, with a visibly shorter cane. It seems that he'd brought it downstairs to the set where carpenters were working, and asked one of them to fix it. Pleased, I thanked him very much.

Marvin was also tolerant when I had to leave early – 6:00 p.m. was considered "early" to leave a production office, as I've mentioned. But I had to go home to feed my cat and do my shot (a little "perk" of having MS). Marvin didn't say a peep as I waved g'bye – mind you, why should he? He knew that often I'd come back afterward, if necessary, to complete whatever task I might have left unfinished.

The Hunger ends

Although *The Hunger* staggered to the finish line, I have to say it gave me a terrific all-round glimpse of film production for television. I had a chance to meet some extraordinary people – directors, actors and crew – and for the most part it was a very positive experience. The show gave me a renewed appreciation for film as a group effort. It honed my own script-coordinating skills. It also nicely paid my rent for over two years.

PART SEVEN – DARK DAYS

I devoted a lot of space to my experience on *The Hunger* not only because it took up two years of my decade in the biz, but also because it gave me some hard-earned grey hairs. Somehow, poking fun at the cause of them makes me feel better.

But it wasn't only *The Hunger* that aged me. Several other shows also gave me the heebie-jeebies. Here are a few – in no particular order.

Bette Midler's defeat – and mine

Isn't She Great? was an ill-conceived biopic feature on the life of author Jacqueline ("Valley of the Dolls") Susann. It starred Bette Midler, badly miscast in the opinion of many. I was called to work on the show while pre-production was in full swing. Handing me the script, the production coordinator asked me if I could have the changes done by the next afternoon. I flipped through it casually ("casually" being the operative word – my first mistake), noting some scribbled lines throughout, I abided by my usual film-biz credo, "Always say yes." So, I said yes.

But I should have said no. Had I looked through the whole script carefully, I would have seen that there was no way I could have input all the changes in less than 24 hours… unless I pulled an all-nighter – and hey, I was too old for that!

So, I got home and started working on it. And worked on it. And worked on it. Truth be told, I was only about 50% done by the next morning, when I realized to my horror that I wasn't going to finish in time for the deadline. The job had been very intricate. There were virtually no lines of dialogue left unchanged; scenes were juggled; headings scrapped, and so on ad infinitum. In truth, this was almost like typing a completely new script, but it took even longer than that because I had to peer at chicken-scratch handwritten notes that looked like they'd been scrawled over one tee-many-martoonies at 4:00 a.m. the morning before. I had badly misjudged how long the job would take, and now I'd have to face some justifiably unhappy people who were impatiently awaiting my output.

I phoned the production coordinator to give her the bad news. I said I'd be bringing in the hard copy as well as the diskette with my work done so far.

I was hoping they could extend the deadline so that I could finish, but no such luck. The coordinator herself wasn't too terribly upset, but the production manager? Yikes, she was livid.

"Why didn't you tell us if you thought you couldn't do it?!"

This, as it turns out, was a refrain I only heard a couple of times during my film/TV decade – it was the downside of "always saying yes." They were the odd instances, very few mind you, when I couldn't quite make the deadline. No one's perfect – but I shouldn't have promised something that I couldn't deliver.

The thing is, though, I'd thought I *could* deliver, in this case. But I'd been too casual when skimming through the script I was handed in the first place. Had I taken more time to really look it over, I'd have realized there was no way to do it in the time allotted. The truth was: I wanted the job. There you have it.

The Ultimate Horror

This was an oddball sort of gig. I was asked to record the timings of shots in a film's rough cut. It sounded like a fun change from my usual grind at the computer, since it would involve playing a movie back on TV using a VCR, and recording the "IN" and "OUT" times of every shot. *And* the footage. The minutes, seconds and feet were stamped at the bottom of the tape and scrolled by quickly as the tape ran.

I'm sure there are *far* more efficient methods to do this digitally now (or probably even back then!), but in 1998 I didn't know any way to do it other than to sit down in front of the TV, slip the tape of *The Ultimate Weapon* (starring Hulk Hogan!) into my VCR, and start it rolling. Whoops! Press stop! Right there! No, er, back up a tad... there! Wait! Stop! No! Ugh!

This was obviously not working. My

VCR was an older model; it was impossible to stop on a dime. Playback just couldn't be controlled precisely enough for my purposes. Also, it was all way too cumbersome for me – to stop and start the VCR as well as type the minutes/seconds in/out plus the shot content!

Even though I set up a nifty template to record all this, I just couldn't do everything by myself. I prevailed upon my dear daughter for assistance. She had a VCR with a special shuttle/jog dial that would let you control playback much more carefully, and she was willing to help me out.

The next day I went to her house, gingerly threading my way up her walk with my laptop, videocassette tape and script in my briefcase. Why "gingerly"? Why "threading"? Well, ice pellets were falling fast, and manoeuvring was starting to become tricky.

Anyway, working with Kathryn was much better… at least in the beginning.

She took on the task of handling the remote: she'd start and stop the tape, and call out the *in* times and *out* times. I'd type those into my template, then look up and see what the shot was portraying, and type a phrase that briefly described it. But it sure was slow going.

Each day for an entire week I'd go over there, braving the icy winds and treacherous sidewalks, falling twice – smack in the middle of Eastern Canada's Ice Storm of the Century.

And all the while, Kathryn and I gradually started to get on each other's nerves. Even though her VCR was more up to the task than mine was, it was still excruciatingly picky work. It didn't help that I was exhausted from schlepping over there each day, and she was going bonkers from being housebound for the week, forced to do this loathsome job, and probably regretting having said "yes" to me!

By the time the work was done, we were hardly on speaking terms – and I couldn't bear to see one more frame of Hulk Hogan's man-tanned face! Not to mention hear some of the corny dialogue that stuck with me like an earworm for weeks, such as:

> Look. You and my dad were partners for fifteen years. All he ever talked about was how you were the best. I think he'd want us to hook up and raise some hell!

I don't think I've ever wished a job to go away more than this one.

****

The Ultimate Weapon – template excerpt

BLACK	01:00:25:13 38.02	01:00:28:12 42.09	MT3 SLIDE TO CENTER FRAME L TO R OVER *HULK HOGAN* [CRUNCH AS NAMES SLIDE TOGETHER]
SLIDING INTO BLACK	01:00:39:21 70.00	01:00:46:21 59.08	MT4 CU SPARKS ZOOM OUT TO REVEAL TITLE CENTER FRAME OVER *THE* *ULTIMATE WEAPON* [SCREECHY METALLIC SOUND][RUSTLING OF LEAVES]
	01:01:01:07 91.13	01:01:03:21 95.08	MT5 CENTER FRAME OVER BLACK *STARRING* *DANIEL PILON*
	01:01:03:22 95.09	01:01:06:06 99.04	MT6 CENTER FRAME OVER BLACK *CARL MAROTTE*
	01:01:06:07 99.05	01:01:08:21 103.00	MT7 CENTER FRAME OVER BLACK *CYNDY PRESTON* [CHILD SCREAMING]

SC.#	TIME/FOOTAGE IN	OUT	DESCRIPTION/DIALOGUE/MUSIC & EFFECTS

[NOTE: FOOTAGE & TIME CODE START 8 SEC. BEFORE FIRST FRAME OF ACTION.]

			REEL ONE A & B
	01:00:00:01 00.00		PICTURE START MARK
	01:00:08:02 12:01		FIRST FRAME OF ACTION
	01:00:08:02 12.01	01:00:11:00 16.07	MT1 CENTER FRAME OVER BLACK
			[MUSIC IN]
			THE JOHN STRONG COMPANY PRESENTS
	01:00:11:01 16.08	01:00:14:00 20.15	MT2 CENTER FRAME OVER BLACK
			A SHOSTAK/ROSSNER PRODUCTION
1.	01:00:14:01 21.00		EXT. FOREST/CLEARING NEAR CLIFF - DAY
			INTERCUT ALL WITH TITLES: IN SLO MO SOFT FOCUS: CAM SHOWS CUTTER RUNNING THROUGH TREES HOLDING GIRL, SOLDIERS CHASING HIM. SOLDIERS FIRE RIFLES AT HIM. CU'S OF RUNNING LEGS. CUTTER WOUNDED. GIRL SLIDES OFF CLIFF. ON CUTTER'S FACE AS SOLDIER IS ABOUT TO SHOOT HIM.
			[FOOTSTEPS IN LEAVES]

…And you're beginning to see what I meant by "picky work"!

Squanto: A Warrior's Tale – the Scriptmeister's lament

Supposedly based on a true story, the blurb for this movie on the IMDb tells the "Tale" best:

"Historically inaccurate chronicle of Squanto's life prior to and including the arrival of the 'Mayflower' in 1620."

Similar to *The Hunger* which came along a few years later, the show would take in, chew up and spit out many crew members due to the chaos that flew about unchecked. For me, it was an extremely difficult gig. The script program I had to use was that software from hell I spoke of in PART THREE – ALLEGRO FILMS. Yes. The dreaded Scriptor.

You may recall that this evil program forced you to start your formatting of the script all over from the beginning, if you made one mistake. This usually occurred when you were at the critical point of locking the pages. You may also recall the *reason* that locking pages is so critical, is so that the top text and bottom text on each page from that point on stays the same from version to version – with the exception of added A & B pages. If you *don't* recall this, it's okay. I didn't warn you a quiz was coming, so you're off the hook!

In any case, I struggled with the program and somehow managed to keep pages locked and my sanity intact. However, script changes abounded. I'd never seen so many before. This made lots of work for me, but it also made all the other production people go bonkers – folks like set designers, builders, prop people, assistant directors, costumers, and on and on... changes upon changes for all of us.

I remember obtaining a giant framed

poster which I impishly erected on the wall over my computer desk: it showed a steely-eyed Clint Eastwood aiming a rifle right out towards you, the viewer, while the caption read: GO AHEAD! MAKE MORE CHANGES!

Squanto was wearing out many crew members, one by one. An assistant director (one of many) came into my office one day, plunked himself down in a chair and put his head in his hands.

"Are... are you okay?" I asked him, concerned. Big sigh.

The next day he was gone.

This was the show I mentioned earlier, in my reminiscences about insecure writers. So, this one particular writer was composing a scene, dictating to me, got stuck, and then took great umbrage at me, the lowly script coordinator, daring to suggest a word. And it was such a good word, too...

Before I get to the *really* unpleasant part, I just want to mention one atypically nice thing that happened. A producer actually praised me one day. Her name was Kathryn Galan. I had just disseminated a set of script revisions, neatly and on time. She looked at me and said, for all around to hear – echoing Rob Schneider's character on *Saturday Night Live* – "Ellie Presnerrr! The Scriptmeisterrr!"

What can I tell you? Kind words were hard to come by.

Okay, now for the worst. The picture was

going to shoot in Louisbourg, Nova Scotia. (This was to capture the feel of coastal Massachusetts centuries ago.)[15] I figured I would be going with them, since no one but me knew how to use the ornery script software. Several people on the production led me to believe that I would indeed be included with the rest of the crew.

I made arrangements for my neighbour to look after my cat, and was starting to pack for a sojourn of two or three months, when the bombshell was dropped: No, I was told, I would *not* be going. Oh? Then who will do the script revisions, I asked. Oh, "Diane" will do them.

Now Diane, I should tell you, was the perky 19-year-old assistant to the director. Did I mention the show had an arty European director... with the emphasis on art? In his mind, I don't think he was making a commercial film; rather he was making a movie that he hoped would garner various prizes at illustrious film festivals around the world, and he would be hailed as a modern-day Antonioni or Fellini, or some such.

The opening shots of the film involved a hawk circling in the sky. Did Arty Director use stock shots? Nope. They had to bring in a hawk and hawk wrangler from who knows where.

So: Diane. Did I mention she was about 19? Did I mention her mini-skirts? NO that's

---

[15] See https://en.wikipedia.org/wiki/Squanto to read about the actual life of this sixteen/seventeenth-century native, Squanto, who helped the pilgrims when they first landed.

not relevant! Forget I said that! *But* - did I mention she was almost computer illiterate? Okay, that last barb is the salient part.

I tried to show her how to copy and paste, on the super-friendly Mac desktop I was using at the time. (It belonged to the production.) Diane could barely master how to move the mouse. This is not a joke.

"Go up to the menu," I had told her, slowlllllyyyy, pointing, while sitting next to her, "and click on Edit. Then go dowwwwwnnnn to Copy..." She stared dumbly at the screen as if the text written there was in, say, Urdu. I actually think this was the first time she'd ever sat at a computer and *touched* a mouse.

Oh. My. God. ...I thought to myself, way before we just said "OMG." This little girl – this non-computer-user person – was going to go to Louisbourg, Nova Scotia, with the director, cast and crew, and do script revisions *in the most non-user-friendly script-revision software known to humankind?*

I had to tell somebody. I did. I told everybody who would listen... but to no avail. They were adamant. Diane was going. I was not. I was to *teach* her how to use the evil program, *Scriptor*. She, who did not even know how to maneuver a mouse, was going to input revisions, master the locking of pages, generate A & B pages, the whole lot – as if by magic.

I did try to teach her, but it was impossible. Not enough understanding of the computer on her part, and not nearly enough time on my part. In fact, the crew were just about ready to depart.

Off they went. And I was off the production now.

Barely a day or so later, my phone rang. Somehow – maybe from an old crew list? – Diane had found my home phone number.

"Can you help me?" she whined. I could hear fear in her voice. "Uh... how can I help you over the phone, Diane?"

"Oh please, just tell me what to do."

I thought for some moments. This was ridiculous. I could not imagine that she'd be able to follow any directions I might give her. She couldn't follow them when I sat next to her, *showing* her what to do. I thought I could try, but it would take a very long time... and I would die of frustration. And do they expect me to do this for free?! They should have taken me with them!

"Well," I told her, "tell 'Lisa' (the production supervisor) that she'll have to pay me. I'll fax her my rate."

"You mean... you won't help me now?"

"I will fax Lisa a contract for her to sign, if she wants me to work over the phone and help you. She has to pay me. Best I can do."

I felt a tad sorry for her as I hung up, yet I was also fuming. Why oh why didn't they take me there, I would never know. I faxed my quote to Lisa. But I never heard back. Only a resounding silence emanated from Louisbourg,

Nova Scotia.

There are two postscripts to this story. The first: I later spoke to a couple of people I knew who had gone on the shoot. Apparently, the weather had been absolutely horrendous. Storms, sea surges, gusts, cold and general misery made for extreme discomfort all around. I didn't feel so bad not having gone, after all.

But the second event made me feel awful. It was maybe a year or so later, and I was working on a show at a large studio where several other shoots were also in pre-production at the same time, in adjacent offices or on different floors. I was leaving the ladies' room just as someone else was opening the door to come in. I came face to face with my nemesis, the unwilling-to-pay-me Lisa!

Caught totally off guard, I gave her a tiny smile and said, "Oh, heh, hi! I guess… you were maybe kind of upset about what happened?"

"I was *furious!!*" she spat, brushing past me.

Yikes. It wasn't my proudest moment. I have to say, though, that my friends at the time backed me during this whole escapade. What are friends for?

Secret Agent Man – a new definition of "crazy"

Note that this show is not to be confused with *Secret Agent,* aka *Danger Man,* the 1964 series starring Patrick McGoohan – the precursor of *The Prisoner*. No, this new production was a pilot being shot here for the same reason many U.S. productions were at the time (1999) – our dollar was really cheap. Producers could get so much more bang for their buck by shooting in Canada. They also benefited from our various government grants and perks. All in all, it truly suited their bottom line to shoot here.

A lot was on the line for this show. The creator/producers from L.A. obviously were hoping the pilot would be as terrific as it could possibly be, so the show would be picked up for a regular season on network TV. Consequently, they chose Montreal as a stand-in for whatever city the actual story took place in – which was standard practice in almost all American productions that came up to Canada. We had (and still have!) excellent production facilities and super crews.

They now had to pry a wonderful *completed* script from the writer's (slightly addled) brain, onto a computer... *my* computer. The deal was this: I had to go to the Omni Hotel every day for about a week and a half, along with my laptop.

Four of us – two producers, the writer and myself – sat facing each other across a giant conference table, in a huge conference room. Every day, we were provided with all the fruit we could eat, gallons of coffee, danish and the like. Cold cuts were brought in for lunch. We sure didn't starve.

I started by importing the script-so-far onto my computer and formatting it in Final Draft. This didn't take long; I could just about do it in my sleep by then.

And then? Now I felt like nodding off, to be honest. The writer sat there, as producers waited on his words to come painfully out of his mouth so I could... type... them... into... the... s c r i p t. I think we may have been gifted with about one or two lines of text per hour, coaxed from this fellow.

Did I mention that this person was assigned a *minder*? (As Wikipedia explains, this is "a term for anyone who looks after the interests of someone or something, such as a talent manager, a caretaker, or a person that ensures that a certain official protocol or plan is adhered to by others, or someone that is designated to look after someone who needs assistance.")

Perhaps you get the picture. Truth be told, I didn't really care that much... the food was yummy, and I was getting paid by the hour! What could be better?!

Finally, after spending several long days getting lines out of this fellow at the speed of molasses on a cold day, the pilot script was more or less complete. Of course, now they wanted to print it. There was just one little problem, however. This was still before the days of major "business centres" in hotels, bursting with computers, printers, copiers, and connectivity galore. The hotel did not have a printer compatible with my Mac laptop. In those days, Macs were still a small minority in the business world; many abounded in the arts, yes; but in business, no.

Finally, I suggested that I could go out to a nearby copy centre that would surely have Mac connectivity, and get the darn thing printed. One of the lower-level producers and I would go together to get this done.

Who knows why I didn't call first; I guess I'm the eternal cock-eyed optimist. (My best friend calls me "Polly" for "Pollyanna"!) It was about 8 p.m. on a lonely dark weeknight, as we trudged, in the wind and spitting rain, to the copy centre a few blocks over on a downtown side street. Nope, they did not have Mac connectivity.

The producer with me – far from the warmth of his native L.A. – was *not* impressed. I believe he was gnashing his teeth at that point, and probably thinking "This is not in my job description!"

But I wasn't impressed either, me, a veritable Mac evangelist as I have mentioned! I was also a tad embarrassed, truth be told. With myself, and my fair city, for permitting this annoying waste of time and energy. At any rate, I saved the day – sort of. I suggested that first thing the next day, we bring in my own Mac printer.

So, at the appointed hour the next morning, a driver was sent to pick me up along with my Mac Laserwriter which, being a *very* heavy, *very* early version I had been given by my ex-husband a few years previously, weighed about as much as a medium-sized elephant. I was glad the driver was strong. The poor guy had to heft this thing down three (albeit short) flights of stairs from my upper flat to his waiting car.

We get to the hotel. I set up the printer and it works. The script prints. Yay.

I enjoyed a few more days' work on this pilot. Everybody was – finally – happy and relieved... except maybe the production manager, to whom I presented my invoice in person at the office when I was finished the gig. She said to me, pointedly, "Thank you for your... *expensive* work." I took the high road and just smiled sweetly.

Although the pilot for *Secret Agent Man* was shot here in Montreal, the series was not. It was picked up, but shot in Vancouver. (Still in cheapo Canada, but without the French factor for unilingual Californians to cope with.) It only lasted twelve episodes.

I am pinched by the Winch

Okay, this was probably my worst script-work experience of all, which is saying a lot.

Largo Winch was a one-hour TV series based on a Belgian comic book; it had a pretty strong cult following.[16] A European-Canadian

---

[16] http://groupwinch.com/home.php

co-production, it was shepherded here mainly by seasoned Montreal producers. The script-coordinating gig came my way via... somebody; I just don't recall who it was. (I think I've blocked it out!)Look, it started off to be very promising. Even though my office area consisted of a teensy corner of a hallway just outside the large office of the producer's assistant, I didn't hold that against them! No, over the years I'd become inured to off-task noises, sights and smells. I'd learned to tune out extraneous stimuli.

The producer's assistant wielded a lot of power on the show, although I certainly didn't begrudge her this, as she was indeed very astute and capable... especially technologically. In fact, she left me behind in the dust, quite frankly. I wasn't completely at ease with the Internet yet. At the production offices I'd been working in up until this point, there was still a whole lotta faxin' going on.

First things first: this assistant, "Marina," (yet another name change to protect the not-so-innocent) introduced me to the main players – two of the exec producers, and three in-house writers. I talked with the writers, and *thought* I established clearly how the script flow would best operate. By this time, I'd already worked on many series, including the craziest, *The Hunger,* and I knew how script versions should be handled – for accuracy, efficiency, and for the good of the show.

But it was all for naught. Scripts flew about willy-nilly. No one person seemed to keep track of which script was at which stage with which writer, and when said script was due! That was *supposed* to be *me*, dammit! But I was completely undermined by the lack of someone (a story editor?!) funneling scripts to me in an organized way. These writers would just plop a draft on a disk and sometimes give it to me, but other times did not. Even when I received one, and dutifully started to proofread and format it properly on my computer, ding ding ding! – *another* version of it came along later in the day from the same writer! He didn't wait for me to give him the "Elliefied" (i.e., fixed) version! This was just impossible.

I voiced my concerns to Marina. She shrugged it off. The writers continued to ignore me. What was I there for, I wondered! Well I'll tell you a couple of things. And they didn't make me feel any better. Marina would order me to print out a script, make a gazillion copies, and distribute them to the dozens of cast and crew members. Now by this time in my career, please understand, this was no longer something I was used to doing. Productions had other staff – usually the production secretary and a production assistant, with the production coordinator overseeing the distribution – to do the work, very time-consuming stuff, which a script coordinator on a series no longer had time to do. But here on this show, since my role had been completely undermined, I was to do these tasks I now found a demeaning chore, to be honest.

But I had way more trouble with another task. Marina instructed me to upload each script version to a certain website so that the co-production partners in Europe would have the latest script drafts. Two problems here: often it wasn't clear just what *were* the latest versions, since I was no longer able to hang on to the crucial role of Keeper of the Scripts.

The second thing was, the uploading took forever on my very old laptop. (I was using my own computer on this show.) And the technical aspects of exactly how/what/where I was to do this were not clear to me. She told me what to do but it somehow didn't jell. (Maybe I felt almost as lost as little Diane, the non- computer-literate 19-year-old pleading for my help on the *Squanto* pic. Ay yi, karma!)

It was a struggle, is what I'm saying. I was very stressed, losing sleep, headachy, you name it. For once, it would be *my* turn to leave a series before my contract ended. I'd never done this before. But for my own sanity it was time to go. Needless to say, Marina wasn't too pleased. But she wasn't pleased with me *anyway*, so I figured I'd just save myself and leave.

Good thing that, by contrast, I'd had some super-great experiences on other shows, which leads me to...

PART EIGHT – THE PLANETS ARE ALIGNED

Some shows were truly a pleasure to work on. With the cooperation and respect among the good-humoured people involved, along with the crackling energy and creative teamwork pervading the productions – these gigs were fulfilling and fun. Here's a random sampling from my film-biz decade.

Loss of Faith (aka The Truth About Lying)

What made this MOW so enjoyable for me were the people with whom I worked most closely. The main collaborators on the film were producers Danièle J. Suissa and Anne Ditchburn. I got along with them famously. I'd briefly worked with Anne once before, but hadn't known Danièle. As a threesome, there was a definite synergy at work, including mutual respect across the board. I was included in script-revising/rewriting sessions – of which there were many.

One memorable working supper took place at their condo. First, we enjoyed a wonderful fish dinner they'd prepared, and then we got down to it. Hours later, satisfied with our revisions, which I'd typed up on my laptop, I left and went home. And a couple of hours after that, I was violently ill. Still green around the gills, I showed up for work the next day somewhat late – but didn't say a word to them about my evening spent alternating between bed and bathroom. No way was I up to asking, "Um... by any chance, were either of you sick as a dog last night?" So, unless they're reading this book, they'll never know. Shh! Don't tell them!

A few weeks later, I attended the table read. It was held in a hotel conference room (I'd seen a lot of them in my career by now), as there wasn't a large enough room where our day-to-day offices were. I had my laptop set up, and as the reading went on, with each actor saying their lines, and everyone contributing changes (minor by this time!), we started to see that the end of the script's journey to shooting-script-readiness was nigh. A sumptuous cold cuts/fruit/rolls etc. buffet was laid out just outside the doors of the room.

I joined the others at the table bursting with food, and looked up to my left to find myself staring into the warm eyes of John Ritter. "Hi," I grinned up at him. "Hi there," he answered, warmly, as he popped red grapes into his mouth. "Nice spread, huh?" I said inanely. Hey, what would *you* have said to John Ritter had you been in my shoes?

We had a pleasant little conversation, but the only thing I recall is that I told him my son had been a huge fan of "Three's Company." He seemed genuinely delighted! I had the feeling he was really happy that the show had reached younger fans as well as an older demographic. (My son was 12 during the show's last season in 1984; he was a big TV fan in general. He's now an editor of TV shows, so all those hours in front of the tube paid off!)

John's demeanour was in stark contrast to the female lead of *Loss of Faith*, Daphne Zuniga. Daphne behaved as though she had lemon rind permanently stuck inside her mouth. 'Nuff said.

The script still went through many small changes after that table read, until finally they petered out. Good thing too: we were all getting kind of tired of the process by now. Like me, they probably knew the darn thing inside out and backwards. I for one was ready to move on.

Heist – Mamet moments

Heist was a David Mamet (*Glengarry Glen Ross; Wag the Dog; Ronin*) flick through and through. Shot in Montreal with many of his regulars, i.e. his wife Rebecca Pidgeon, Ricky Jay, Richard Friedman and others, as well as Gene Hackman and Danny DeVito, it was the highest-profile film shooting in town that season.

(It was only much later that I noticed one of the exec producers as well as the line producer were the same ones as on my woeful 1994 gig, *Squanto: A Warrior's Tale*, wherein I earned the ire of the producer's assistant. But thankfully our paths never crossed this time.)

I worked from home on this show, so to my disappointment, I didn't get to meet the great man himself, Mamet, who had a rep as someone rather idiosyncratic and unapproachable.

Instead, his revised lines were fed to me over the phone by his usual first AD, Cas Donovan. She called him "Dave." Given a second title of co-producer, she usually read the notes to me while taking her dog on walks; it made for a rather surrealistic experience – suitable for a Mamet flick, I suppose. (By the way, it wasn't unusual for crew or cast members to bring their dogs to work, since their hours were so long.) If I ever questioned anything in the revisions, Cas would inevitably say, nicely, "No, Dave wants it this way…" I suppose it's silly, but somehow I always found it hard to imagine David Mamet as a "Dave"! To me, a "Dave" was a Letterman, or maybe a guy in a baseball cap at a Red Sox game.

The other method of receiving "Dave's" script revisions was by fax. His lines would peel through on my fax machine, curled up on the thermal paper of the day – and when I unfurled the page I'd be greeted by single-spaced typewritten rows, all bunched up together near the top, complete with x'd-out and gummed-up letters, as if the keys had stuck together. Quite a low-tech presentation, shall we say. But the man sure knew whereof he wrote.

Jackie O.

Jacqueline Bouvier Kennedy Onassis, the show we crew members knew fondly as *Jackie,* was a TV mini-series filmed mostly in Montreal. Since it was a very big shoot, I shared duties with another script coordinator – whom I never met, as we worked on site on different days.

The thing I enjoyed most on this show was the feeling of being truly appreciated by the producers. One of them even said he wished I could come to L.A. and work with him there on future productions. I figured he was just saying that to be nice, though. Why did I think this? Wellll… I gave him my card but he never called me. (Besides, I'm sure L.A. was – and still is – crawling with script coordinators. Also, these days, with much friendlier software available, many writers or their assistants can do their own revisions.)

He and a co-producer often expected me (and my laptop!) to hang out with them as they were brainstorming changes to scenes, dialogue and so on. The most memorable were the times they came over to my home office as we sat around casually and discussed scenes. Every once in a while, one or the other of them would yell, "Yes! Put that in!!" And dutifully, I would. It was fun viewing the creative process up close; this was always my favourite part of the job.

Once during a session at my place, we all

got hungry and felt like going out to eat. We went to a nearby chain restaurant, Nickel's (once owned by Celine Dion and Rene Angélil). In a booth, in between munching good ol' American-type deli food, they hashed out lines, and I, with my trusty Mac PowerBook, like to think I helped.

Another time, one of those two producers – George Stelzner – had a driver bring me out to the set, in a posh suburb of Montreal, all verdant and leafy – a perfect stand-in for Hyannis. He set me up in a trailer with my laptop, and between each shot, he'd pop in and feed me revised lines to type. This was fun except for one thing – a metal trailer gets awfully hot in the noonday sun.

Sherlock Holmes!

Director Rodney Gibbons was one of my favourite film people to work with. Not a speck of hubris in him that I could detect, this man embodied humility, one of the personality aspects I truly admire in a person. I knew of him back when I worked at Allegro Films; he was often the preferred director of cinematography on their shows.

But now that he'd moved up to director status on a bunch of Sherlock Holmes remakes for Muse Entertainment, and I was script coordinator, we shared office space on these two shows. (Had I stayed on in the business, I'm sure I would have worked with him on many more shows after the Holmes batch. My loss.)

The screenwriter for *Hound of the Baskervilles* and *The Royal Scandal* (aka *Scandal in Bohemia*), Joe Wiesenfeld, fed me revisions by phone or fax, and I kept track of all sets of changes as usual.

It was only a bit later in the process, once Joe's role was over, that Rodney felt the need to do some bits of revisions on his own. These were usually necessitated by changes of shooting locations and the like. He would dictate his changes to me verbally, slowly, as I typed them in on my laptop... Occasionally I would suggest what I thought was a better word or phrase, and he'd immediately like it. In a teensy way, once again, I felt part of the creative process.

These Sherlock shoots also had Pedro Gandol as first AD, and I loved working with him too. We'd been on many of the same shows, including the two-parter, *Revenge of the Land; The Audrey Hepburn Story;* and *Heart, the Marilyn Bell Story.*

Caillou's Corner

Having worked on a lot of Cinar productions by now, I was a known entity to them... and so at the start of 2000, the call came for me to work on a new version of this long-running animated children's series. Caillou is a cute little boy we see learning about the world, while preschool viewers learn along with him.

For some reason, the powers-that-be had decided to tweak a successful concept by adding live-action skit-and-song segments with puppets in between the pre-shot animated parts; this newly reconstituted show was to be aired on PBS. My role as script coordinator was to keep track of all versions of some 40 puppet/song scripts.

Each script was short, as the puppet segments ran no more than a few minutes at most. I was also responsible for creating episode breakdowns, with timings noted. Here's only *part* of a sample:

CAILLOU'S CORNER
"Getting Along"- #138 - First Draft
Episode Segments – Breakdown

	Segment	Time	Total acc. time
1	PBS - VLY	0:10	
2	Show Opening	1:00	
3	PUPPETS Segment – Scene 1 Int. Bedroom: Rexy comes in as Gilbert and Teddy are concentrating on their chess game. He tries various ways to engage their attention, but they shush him.		
4	TRANSITION: 1/2 bridge extro to black A flower vase sits on a table, as we... Wipe to:		
5	Animation Segment – "Caillou's Cross Word" - #138 Caillou uses a mean word he learned when playing with Clementine. This hurts her feelings, so Mom gets Caillou to apologize to her, and then they're friends again.	3:15	
6	TRANSITION: 1/2 bridge intro from black A flower vase sits on a table and the table moves back and forth, as we... Wipe to:		
7	PUPPETS Segment – Scene 2 Int. Bedroom: Rexy's still hanging around Gilbert and Teddy while they play chess. Suddenly he sneezes a huge sneeze which makes the chess board and pieces go flying, just as Gilbert is about to make a great move. Gilbert is very angry with Rexy.		
8	TRANSITION: 1/2 bridge extro to black A flower vase sits on a table and the table moves back and forth, the vase cascades to the floor, a child's voice says 'sorry' as we... Wipe to:		
9	Animation Segment – "Caillou's Promise" - #141 Caillou keeps a promise even though it's not easy; his reward is a circus visit!	7:00	
10	TRANSITION: 1/2 bridge intro from black A screen door is closed, as we... Wipe to:		
11	PUPPETS Segment - Scene 3 Ext. Backyard: Rexy's very sad because Gilbert got angry with him. He tells Teddy that he thinks Gilbert should apologize to him for getting so angry earlier. Teddy tries to explain to Rexy why Gilbert got mad. Rexy still feels he's the 'victim.'		
12	TRANSITION: 1/2 bridge extro to black A screen door is open, as we... Wipe to:		
13	Animation Segment –"Caillou's New Friend" - #38 Caillou doesn't like the new boy, Jim, he meets in the park at first, but with a bit of intervention from Caillou's Grandpa and Jim's mom, they learn to play well together.	3:15	

The missing timings were added in later; the total would add up to 30 minutes.

I also kept up a script-delivery schedule and organized all the song lyrics while of course keeping all the versions straight. As I was on staff and went to work every day at the huge loft they'd rented, I was able to collaborate closely with the writer, Mary Mackay-Smith, as well as the assistant production manager, Marie-Josée Ferron. It was a fun gig: my colleagues were super-nice people, and the content of each episode was very sweet in tone as well as educational... somewhat reminiscent of Sesame Street.

Cirque du Soleil

What cachet that title holds! When I got the call in the summer of 2000, I positively trembled with anticipation. Luckily the timing for me was perfect – my *Caillou* gig had just wrapped – and I was free to get on board.

For my "hiring interview" I was invited to go to the Cirque's headquarters at 8400 2nd Avenue in the Saint-Michel district of Montreal, some 40 minutes or so from my home. I would gladly have driven 40 hours.

As I approached the property, it was a sight to behold. The buildings occupy many acres, and the ample parking lots overflow with cars. It was certainly the most enormous complex bearing a single address that I'd ever seen – aside from an airport!

The production manager of the planned TV show gave me a tour, including the offices, various workshops and soaring rehearsal space, after which we sat down to discuss the show and my role in it. I looked around, impressed by the large, airy cafeteria, screened in on all sides and topped with a huge skylight to boot.

I learned that the broadcast/production division of the Cirque was now planning a TV series; the concept was a variety show consisting of Cirque skits interspersed with bits by stand-up comedians. I would be known as a "writer's assistant" and *de facto* script coordinator. Since I was in on the ground floor so to speak, I got to see the development of a unique show almost from the beginning.

Our production offices were to be located in the huge broadcasting complex known as the TVA building, just east of the downtown core of Montreal. TVA is a mostly French-speaking conglomerate, encompassing all sorts of TV production facilities, including sound stages, editing suites, offices, and the like. It would be these facilities that the show would use during its run.

To call our production "unique" would be an understatement. It was, well... bizarre. You know those Cirque skits involving clowns, or a hat stand, or other ethereal beings, backed by haunting music and featuring droll-yet-sad-or-wistful overtones? No? Well anyway, these were exactly like that!

Several experienced Canadian writers had been hired, including a well-known fellow in the biz named John Boni, who was also the supervising producer. Boni had cut his teeth writing for a long succession of successful TV series, and was now tasked with developing ideas together with the writers under his wing, and shepherding them (the ideas!) from outline to rough draft through all versions right up to the final.

I was along for the ride, collecting drafts, distributing them to all concerned, and keeping the versions organized snugly in my computer.

Working on this particular show was very enjoyable, as the writers were all entertaining and friendly. I became quite close with the woman who was the assistant to the executive producer; she became my pal/comrade-in-arms for the duration. I also liked the logistics coordinator who sat at the desk across from mine, and had a penchant for Edith Piaf; many of our working hours were accompanied by the lusty strains of "Non, je ne regrette rien" and "La vie en rose" coming from her portable CD player.

I did not play any part in the hiring of stand-up comedians for the bits that would be sprinkled in and around the Cirque skits. However, there was one tiny task I *was* asked to do. When one particular aspiring comedy star showed up for his audition, he went straight to the sign-in desk downstairs in the cavernous TVA lobby and announced his business to the kiosk attendant. The attendant in turn rang us upstairs, to tell us of the comedian's arrival. The producer then asked me – (Why me? – who knows! I was available?) – to go down and fetch the fellow and bring him up to our offices. This was *way* preferable to the kiosk attendant having to instruct the visitor how the heck to find us through a veritable maze of hallways, elevators and dead ends. He could have become lost, never to be heard from again. (The next day's *Montreal Gazette* might have blared: "Local Comedian Disappears in TVA Production Offices! Hope Fading." The sub-head might have said, "Cirque Show To Be a Tad Less Funny.")

Actually, what struck me as I shook the visitor's sweaty hand and led him through the jungle of corridors to our offices was how particularly unfunny he was. In fact, he was downright morose. *Depressed*, it seemed to me. He looked like he was going to his doom. I tried to lighten the mood by asking him nonchalant questions, and even tried cracking a few modest jokes myself... but to no avail. The alleged funnyman was not having any of it. I'd heard of stage fright, but... well... whatever. I led him to his doom – I mean, to the fancy corner office of one of the executive producers, and left him there, shivering. Poor guy.

So, things were running along smoothly, from my vantage point: writers were writing... producers were producing... production designers were designing... comedians were being comical (well, except for that last guy)... all was right with the world... and then –

One day the executive producer, Peter Wagg, let us know he wanted to meet with everyone. This was rather unusual. At noon, we all gathered in the open area, near the little kitchen. We sat on the carpeted floor to await Peter's news. With great sadness, this award-winning producer reluctantly told us that production on our show was being suspended. He did not give us any reason, just that things were not working out, he was *terribly* sorry, but that was it. And so, we had to pack it in. (This was just before sets were to be built, so I suppose the money people were glad they'd at least saved *that* expense.)

I had never experienced anything like this during my decade in the biz; it was rather shocking. Ironically, earlier that week, the prospective name for the show – to which much attention had been paid, with suggestions requested from all employees – had finally been decided upon. It was: *Basta!* Which is Italian for: *Enough!*

PART NINE – EXTRAS

Interspersed with features and series I've already talked about, were various gigs that were in a class by themselves: multi-part mini-series, documentaries, French productions, script analyses, and some one-offs, i.e. one-day wonders, as I thought of them.

Minis

Dice – a mini-series comprising six parts, and *Random Passage*, an eight-parter, afforded me months of solid work. Occasionally I'd go down to the production offices for meetings, but mostly laboured on my computer at home, neatly placing each episode's printed-out revised pages in separate piles (Pink! Blue! Green!) on my carpeted home-office floor. I always liked to have hard copies of the revisions, if only so I could see exactly what the people on the production would be getting. I also found it more effective to proofread on paper than on the screen.

After a while I bought a long camper table to hold the multi-coloured script piles, marching in rows down its length. (I had a hard time keeping my cat off them – he so liked to lie on anything papery!)

On most mini-series I was not expected to do the dissemination; the production coordinator and her staff took care of it. I would just email my updated versions to their office. *Tant mieux,*

as they say in French! *So much the better.*
Distributing all the script copies was never my
most cherished duty. No, what I enjoyed most
was the formatting, editing and proofreading of
the text. My goal was always to make the
writers look good – or even better than they
already did.

Speaking of *Dice*, I'm reminded of another
of my favourite parts of the film biz – the wrap
parties! As I've mentioned elsewhere, these
were usually rollicking affairs in an ultra-trendy
setting, with a live band or at least a great DJ to
get the crowd dancing.

Since I am not a natural extrovert, I'd often
manage to banish my jitters with a drink – or
two. That is my only excuse for what I did at
the *Dice* wrap party.

Early in the evening, before things got
noisier and crazier, as I was on my second
drink and starting to feel quite… mellow, shall
we say, idly meandering about the room – I
suddenly came face to face with one of the
stars of the series.

The actor's name was Callum Keith
Rennie. Do take a moment now to look him up.
What you have to know is this: his photos don't
do him justice. I can attest to the fact that, in the
year 2000, up close, Callum Keith Rennie
looked like a Greek god.

So I said, "Hi! You were great as 'Egon
Schwimmer'"![17] And I continued, blurting

---

[17] His character in Dice.

enthusiastically, "You... you are one of the most *stunning* men I've ever seen!"

I swear he had the grace to blush. He also looked down, away, off to the side, anywhere but right at me, smiled broadly, and mumbled a thank you. He was very sweet as we continued chatting for another couple of painful minutes. (I told him about my script-coordinator role on the show. I'm not sure he cared but he looked as though he did. Actors!) Finally, I left him alone and beat a retreat, embarrassed at my rather crass, fan-like behaviour.

Docs

For a change of pace, I enjoyed working on documentary scripts. Sometimes I did only formatting; other times proofreading, timings and so on. These shows would eventually air on educational TV networks such as PBS. I recall a couple of adventure-laden, interesting scripts written by Josh Freed, a respected Montreal journalist and filmmaker. One story was about a hunt for buried treasure in the Caribbean Sea; another was about the Vikings. This work came my way as part of a series of gigs for a local documentary production company.

I also had an assignment from Morag Productions, a Newfoundland-based company headed by filmmaker Barbara Doran. Barbara gave me the opportunity to rewrite some of the narration for a documentary on the Innu of northern Quebec. Unfortunately, I don't see the production listed at all on her page at IMDb.com… I hope it wasn't something I said!

One thing I remember well about the Innu documentary is the wrap party – which was a dinner hosted by Barbara at Morag's Montreal office, and which featured the *pièce de résistance* (cooked by the star of the show himself, an Innu man): caribou. I sheepishly admit that its strong flavour didn't appeal to me – but the others ate it with gusto!

Productions françaises

So how does an anglo script coordinator/ editor/proofreader/formatter work on scripts that are in French?

Very carefully! Usually it just involved reformatting them, i.e. converting them from a Word file into a file in either Final Draft or Screenwriter software.

Occasionally I happened to spot errors, and corrected them.

Some of the French-language scripts that came my way were TV series; others were features. They included: *15-02-1839; Tribu; Their Last Chance* (shot in both English and French versions); *Faux Pas; Le Voleur de Chiens; Station Nord Ho! Ho! Ho!;* and *Gypsies*. I enjoyed the linguistic change of pace these shows offered.

Script critiques

I found myself doing several script critiques for a new film company, whose president I knew from having worked with her previously at another production house where she'd been a first AD. The scripts had been submitted to her on spec, and she was simply too busy to read them to see if they had potential, so she passed them along to me. One of them in particular was memorable – but not in a good way!

The story consisted entirely of a cat-and-mouse type chase, wherein the bad guy was intent on killing the heroine, and went after her throughout the nooks and crannies of a high-rise building. It was supposed to be brimming with suspense. In my imagination I could just about hear the ominous, shuddering violins signifying imminent evil at every turn. It *should* have been brimming with suspense.

Unfortunately, there were so many plot holes, all of which I painstakingly pointed out, on page after page, that killed any moment of would-be tension. Mostly, said plot holes consisted of Bad Guy catching up to Heroine, and engaging in useless conversation with her, while aiming his gun at her at point- blank range. My frequent notations in my pages-long critique said, unambiguously, WHY DOESN'T HE JUST SHOOT HER NOW?! Of course, the answer was painfully obvious. There would have been no story... and no movie. Here's how

I summed up my analysis:

The number one thing that <u>really</u> bothered me:

1)   WHY HE DOESN'T SHOOT HER IN THE 1,257 CHANCES HE HAS?

Okay, there I exaggerate...slightly, but I do it to make a point. Speaking of points – perhaps a change of weapon would solve this problem. What if his weapon of choice is a knife? Or an icepick?? After all – come to think of it – a gunshot is extremely loud! I can't imagine a professional killer calling attention to his executions that way. True, he could attach a silencer. But then you're back to the problem of WHY DOESN'T HE SHOOT HER...etc. I'm partial to the icepick, myself.

In short: if we fix the premise, modify the characters, change the weapon, improve the dialogue, plug the plot loopholes, spruce up the ending... we won't have an Oscar-winning script but at least it'll be less flawed. Is it worth the time, effort and money?

****

Need I tell you that no movie was ever made from that godforsaken script?

As for other scripts I critiqued negatively for this company, some of them *were* made into (awful) films anyway. There's just no accounting for taste, I suppose.

One-offs

As the heading implies, these types of gigs often involved just one day's work, usually formatting a script once and emailing it back to the production coordinator, first AD, production manager, or whoever had sent it to me.

One day I was brought a script, *Eisenstein* (aka *The Furnace*), a "biopic" about the brilliant Russian filmmaker, Sergei Eisenstein (considered the father of cinematic montage techniques). The movie had already been shot. The person who came to my house was the woman who'd done continuity on it: she wanted me to incorporate all the notes she had scrawled during the shoot on her script copy into the computer file of the script, which her office had sent me. Good thing she sat beside me the whole time. Her writing was almost indecipherable – quite often even to her!

We laboured a total of 10 hours spread over three days – and my invoice looked like this:

Final script revisions & final reformatted/proofed script ("The Furnace" - working title)

Date	Hours	Amount
May 12-14, 2000	10 hr. @ $35	$350.00

TOTAL:	10 hr. @ $35	**$350.00**

Nice work if you can get it. And I did!

A quick word about star power

It's a small coincidence that, of all the scripts I worked on, the two movies starring the biggest A-list actors both had the word "money" in the title. *Where the Money Is* was an offbeat little film starring Paul Newman as a sly, elderly criminal placed in a nursing home. (The writer, E. Max Frye, was later to write *Foxcatcher*, which was nominated for five Academy Awards.)

Free Money, a rather silly comedy, starred Marlon Brando as a goofy prison warden. While doing the *very* frequent script revisions for this show, I'd often hear complaints from people working on set about Brando's penchant for constant script changes on the fly. Apparently, he drove everyone crazy. (Of course, *I* didn't mind, as it was more work for me – and I got paid by the hour!)

Paul Newman, on the other hand, was known as a very nice man, a pussycat to work with.

It takes all kinds.

PART TEN – FADE TO BLACK

End of an era

By 2001 the (script)writing was on the wall. Production companies here started to collapse. The dissolution of most of these creative powerhouses meant the end of the line in the field for many people, including me. Some of the dead and dying companies were Téléscene, Cinar, SDA, Cinévideo, Cité-Amérique, Taurus 7, Allegro and Cinémaginaire.

Not only were there fewer sources of work for me due to these closures, but I also faced another obstacle: there were now several other people doing the same type of script work that I'd been doing practically solo (at least in English) for years, in Montreal – so I had competition for the very few TV series that were still being produced here. In addition, many producers' and directors' assistants on feature films had learned how to do script revisions. Luckily for them, the specialized software had become much simpler and more intuitive by this time. I was a luxury they couldn't afford.

Fade out

After months of job-searching, I finally found a full-time job in a completely different field. It was at a non-profit organization where perfect written and spoken French was, fortunately for me, not an absolute requirement – unlike most other workplaces in Montreal.

I knew I was well and truly out of the film biz when I received a call on my cell phone during my first week on the new job.

"Hello?" I said.

"Hi Ellie! How are you?" It was Jacqueline Marleau – the production coordinator from 1997's *Hysteria*, who had matched me up with Patrick McGoohan to work with him on his *Prisoner* filmscript.

She wondered if I was available to do script revisions on a new film. "Oh," I told her, I would've loved to – but you're a bit too late!"

"What – what do you mean?"

"I had to find a full-time job, Jacqui. The film work just wasn't there. I had to pay the rent, you know?"

She seemed shocked, and tried at first to cajole me into doing the revisions in my "spare time"… but I soon made her understand that this was, unfortunately out of the question. (I knew the ins and outs of script-revision work; the way it could invade your life time-wise, it just wasn't doable. Finally, she saw that I was resolute in my "just saying no." (It was one of the very few times that I broke my film-world rule of "Always say yes.")

After we sadly said good-bye, I realized it was indeed the end of an era for me.

So you want to be a script coordinator?

Let's suppose that after reading all this, you decide you want to be another Ellie Presner. (Heaven help you!) I would humbly suggest, based on my decade of experience in that crazy business, that you read and take to heart the following:

- Seriously consider (if you are intent on remaining in Canada) moving to Toronto or Vancouver. Montreal can no longer be considered "Hollywood North," unless your French is perfect, in which case you may find steady work.
- You need to be flexible. You have to be able to turn on a dime and not be thrown by *changes*, as change is inherent in the business, especially in the role of script coordinator/script revisor. Your main activity is, after all, inputting revisions – i.e. *changes* – into the script.
- You need an excellent command of the English language. Your grammar and spelling should ideally be perfect, and you should have a keen knack for proofreading and consistency. Most of all,

you should *enjoy* what I call the icky-picky business of putting the right words in the right order on the right pages. It's a finicky job. But *somebody's* gotta do it.

Goodbye gifts

As my own little good-bye gift to all you patient readers, I would like to share a list of some of the souvenirs we crew members received when various productions wrapped. Usually the gifts were mainly symbolic or even hokey, and were probably obtained by the film companies at minimal cost. They were fun nevertheless:

- Fleece vest – At the end of *Barney's Great Adventure,* imagine our "delight" when we each received a black fleece vest featuring a huge purple Barney adorning the back. Not that I ever wore it: if the embarrassment of silly Barney weren't enough, the edges of the material were permanently curled. It was unwearable – but it was the thought that counted. Wasn't it?
- Felt scarf – After *Space Cases,* each of us was presented with a grey scarf bearing the colourful logo of the "Starcademy" – which was the astronaut-type training school attended

by the teen heroes and heroines in the show. The gift was kind of neat... if you were a kid.

- Large blue die – No, you read that right. Upon the wrap of the *Dice* miniseries, we were each given a die – a heavy three-inch cube, which could be a cool paperweight, I suppose. It says DICE on it along with the names of the producing partners. It sits on my desk as an excellent dust-catcher.

- Hats – Ball caps, berets, you name it – from productions too numerous to name. I confess they've all found their way to clothing-castoff venues.

- T-shirts – A few times we received T-shirts. One of them, which I still have, stands out particularly for its snarkiness, especially in light of what was to happen down the road. Upon the wrap of *The Hunger* series, we each received a T-shirt that mocked the director, Tony Scott, mercilessly. On the front of the black shirt is a bright pink-and-yellow cartoon drawing of a man, supposedly Tony, with a couple of his affectations exaggerated terribly: He has a humongous cigar jutting from his mouth, a pink ball cap and a distinctly unshaven face. Under this it says HUNGER 99. Above the mean caricature is proclaimed, in pink writing, "I survived Tony Scott." This apparently referred to some difficulties crew members had had with him on the set, but it turned out to be an unwittingly sad and ironic statement, considering that the poor man took his own life some years later.

Looking back at my decade in the film business, I'd have to say the greatest gift that I ever received was the opportunity to have a fascinating niche job, in an exciting, creative milieu where I (almost always!) felt appreciated and completely at home. Great years. Thanks for letting me share my memories with you.

APPENDIX

Filmography

[Note: Many of the shows I was involved with are not listed in my IMDb (Internet Movie Database) entry. Here is a complete listing, in alphabetical order, of shows on which I worked from 1992 to 2001.]

15.02.1839
Aftermath
Aventures dans le Grand Nord (aka Tales of the Wild)
Barney's Great Adventure
Caillou
Captive
Cirque du Soleil
Dead Silent
Diary of an Innu Child
Dice
Eisenstein (aka The Furnace)
Faux Pas
Free Money
Goin' to Kansas City
Gypsies
Heart – The Marilyn Bell Story
Heist
Hound of the Baskervilles
Isn't She Great
Jackie Bouvier Kennedy Onassis
Ladies Room
Largo Winch (2001 TV series)

Le Voleur de Chiens
Little Men
Loss of Faith (aka The Truth About Lying)
Musketeers Forever
Ocean Warrior
Origin of Species
Paradox
Random Encounter
Random Passage
Redeemer
Requiem for Murder
Revenge of the Land
Running Home
Savage Messiah
Scandal in Bohemia (aka The Royal Scandal)
Screamers
Secret Agent
Space Cases
Squanto (aka Indian Warrior)
Station Nord Ho! Ho! Ho!
Stork Derby
Tales of the Wild: Esperanza, Kazan, Baree
The Audrey Hepburn Story
The Edge
The Hunger
Their Last Chance
The Minion
The Paper Boy
The Prisoner
The Secret Pact (2001)
The Unconcerned (aka No Alibi)
The Wrong Woman
Tribu

The Ultimate Weapon
Vendetta II: The New Mafia
Where the Money Is
Witchboard III
Xchange

Script Lore – The Mystery of A & B Pages

Okay: suppose you have one page of a script. Now, suppose the first AD comes to you and says, *We've added a few lines to Melissa's dialogue. Here they are.* She hands you a napkin. It is, miraculously, devoid of stains. *We need them ASAP.* She may or may not say thanks... depending how frazzled she is. (Hint: she's always frazzled.)

At the computer, you navigate to the current file of the script. You find the lines of dialogue to be changed. You insert the new lines. OOPS. Now, you see what just happened there? You don't? Okay, I'll tell you, since you're new. When you added those lines, it pushed all the subsequent lines down onto the next page.

And if you look on the next page, you'll see – horror of horrors! – that everything there has overflowed onto the page after that, too!

Trust me when I tell you: this CANNOT happen. One of the reasons is that cast and crew members have a habit of making notes to themselves on the script.

They jot down memos to themselves, like

Don't forget to smile ironically. Or *Find miniature pony for the child's Xmas gift.* The script pages must retain their numbering, i.e. be *locked,* from the time the production (shooting, table) draft is launched.

So how can the pages *stay* locked, if words are added, or, heaven forbid, omitted? (Whole scenes are often omitted!) The secret is: A & B pages.
Whoever invented those should get a medal. What you do is, you type in those added lines of dialogue given to you by the frazzled AD. And the lines on the page do spill over to the next page. You peek there, and behold!! There are only a few lines that spilled over!! Why? Because earlier, you remembered the rule: LOCK THE PAGES as soon as the production draft is approved.

In those old days of manual page locking, you did it by inserting a "hard" page break wherever you wanted the page to end. That meant a *lot* of manual page-break insertions, in a script of over 100 pages. In later years, there would be special software which would do the locking of the entire script at once when you entered the command. (Very obliging of it.)

Locking pages means that forever after, the

text that is written at the TOPS of each page
will always stay the same… with the exception
of the A & B pages. I've lost you, I can tell.
Here's a (*very*) simplified example.

Let's pretend that each of the following
script pages can only hold three lines in total.
At the start, they look like this [Fig. 1]:

Page 1

```
This is a crazy
script, not much room.
Only three lines on each
page.
```

Page 2

```
I know, it's a bit crazy.
But it's the film biz.
Whatddyagonnado.
```

[Fig. 1]

Okay. Now along comes the frazzled AD and
gives you changes to insert on Page 1. They
happen to consist of four lines:

```
I've seen much longer
ones. Circus World had
520 pages.
I fell asleep typing it.
Good thing this is much
```

```
shorter.
```

Ms. AD wants you to insert these lines after the current second line on Page 1 that ends with "`not much room.`" You go ahead and type them in, putting an asterisk in front of each new line. Now, if you had NOT locked the pages, you would end up with this:

Page 1

```
This is a crazy
Script, not much room.
*I've seen much longer
ones.
```

Page 2

```
*Circus World had 520
pages.
*I fell asleep typing it.
*Good thing this is much
shorter.
```

Page 3

```
Only three lines on each
page. I know, it's a bit
crazy.
But it's the film biz.
```

Page 4

```
Whatddyagonnado.
```

[Fig. 2]

Horrors! You see how everything below the
new lines got shifted down [Fig. 2]? This is
NOT good. The answer is to LOCK pages,
which will produce what are called A & B
pages – although B etc. may not always be
necessary – it depends how much is added.
With *locked* pages, when you enter the added
lines you will get this [Fig. 3]:

Page 1

```
This is a crazy
Script, not much room.
*I've seen much longer
ones.
```

Page 1A

```
*Circus World had 520
pages.
*I fell asleep typing it.
*Good thing this is much
shorter.
```

Page 1B

```
Only three lines on each
page.
```

Page 2

```
I know, it's a bit crazy.
But it's the film biz.
Whatddyagonnado.
```

[Fig. 3]

…And Page 2 is kept untouched, just as it was at the moment the pages were locked, which is exactly what you want.

(I should mention that in those bad old days prior to specialized script-formatting software, I had to put the page numbers in manually. That was the only way to generate a number like 1A, then 1B, and then continue from page number 2 on the next page, as in [Fig. 3].)

Now when you distribute the revised pages to people, in this example you only have to give them Page One plus the A & B pages, since they are the only pages that have changed or are new. If you hadn't locked the pages, you'd have to send out the entire 100-plus-page script every time it changed, since all the text from the new stuff onward was moved down. That's way too many trees!

The cast and crew can easily see the changes, especially since there's an asterisk in the margin next to all changed or deleted lines. In my early days in the trenches, I had to manually put them in, but the amazing software that came along later puts them in automatically. Sigh. Next, we'll have scripts that write themselves... right?

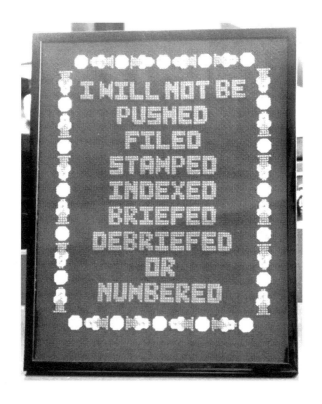

The Prisoner Ethos

My Note re Prisoner Script Scene Headings

SUBJECT: The Prisoner screenplay
Ellie Presner
Jerell Publishing
FAX/VOICE: (514) xxx-xxxx
FAX:xxx-xxx-xxxx

TO: Whomever is using Ellie's MAC disk

DATE: June 27, 1996

Hi, there! A few notes about The Prisoner script. It's in Word 5.1a. And it's all in Courier bold.

The underlining used for scene headings isn't done in the conventional way, because we found the lines to be too flush underneath the characters. Therefore, I figured out another way (mighty convoluted, but here it is):

1) Press Return after typing new scene heading.
2) Choose Scene Head Underline from styles.
3) Press tab.
4) "Draw" an underline under the scene heading, using the underline key (shift-hyphen).
5) Highlight the underline.
6) Press command-D and choose Superscript

3 pts.

7) Highlight just the paragraph mark at the end of the underline.

8) Press command-M, and where it says Line, choose Exactly; type 2 pts. In box.

The Word settings on the disk should replace your Word settings in the System preferences folder.

The Village font files should go in your fonts folder. (This font produces the logo on the title page.) You will need to have ATM installed for it to look right.

And that's it. If any questions or problems, please don't hesitate to call me.

Ellie

(Note from present-day Ellie: I soon made a macro for this underline business, so I wouldn't have to go through the process every time!)

PHOTOS from my Prisoner sojourn *with Patrick McGoohan*

The setup in my motel suite. Patrick snaps a photo of me using my camera. I wasn't ready and let him know!

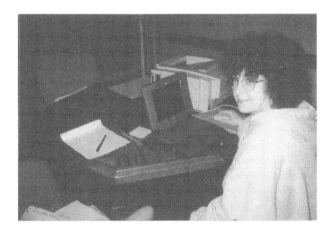

Okay, that's a bit better.

Patrick across from me, mulling over his
Prisoner script.

Patrick strikes an imperious pose at the gate
to his home in Carmel.

Sitting on the patio of his house.
He seems to like me!

Whatever he said, it made me chuckle!

Patrick and his beautiful daughter, Frances.

Patrick and his wife, Joan have a word…

Patrick and Joan relaxing – fittingly, in a
loveseat.

Patrick next to his CD collection, his
granddaughter Nina nearby.

His antique word processor.

In the kitchen, Patrick poses sternly with a
book about money.

Perusing the grandkids' artwork on the fridge
"gallery."

Joan and I let Patrick know we both think
he's a mischievous man.

ACKNOWLEDGEMENTS

I owe a giant debt of thanks to Shane Simmons, Jeremy Presner, John Boone and other readers for their invaluable feedback; to my children and their spouses, and author Dan Alatorre, for their boundless encouragement and belief in me; and to my fans everywhere including my friends and social-media followers who are legion, and who will all run out and buy this book pronto. Or maybe you already did. If so, I humbly thank you.

ABOUT THE AUTHOR

Ellie Presner is a Montreal writer, editor, and former script coordinator. Her blog, https://crossedeyesanddottedtees.wordpress.com has drawn thousands of readers from 102 countries.

Ellie has written, edited, and proofread for a large variety of publications, but the high point of her career is the nomination she received for a National Magazine Award for "Taking Back the Night," which was reprinted in *Essays: Patterns and Perspectives* by Oxford University Press. She still gets a charge out of the fact that her name is just above Bertrand Russell's in the Table of Contents.

When not feverishly working at her Mac, Ellie may be found ensconced in her recliner with her fluffy long-haired cat, Annie, glued to her lap.

72710761R00122

Made in the USA
San Bernardino, CA
29 March 2018